DATE DUE

DE 18 99			
DE 17 04			

DEMCO 38-296

CAMPUS HATE-SPEECH CODES
AND TWENTIETH CENTURY ATROCITIES

George Anastaplo

Symposium Series
Volume 44

The Edwin Mellen Press
Lewiston • Queenston • Lampeter

Library of Congress Cataloging-in-Publication Data

Anastaplo, George, 1925-
   Campus hate-speech codes and twentieth century atrocities / George
Anastaplo.
      p. cm. -- (Symposium series ; 44)
   Includes bibliographical references.
   ISBN 0-7734-8847-2
   1. Discrimination in higher education--United States. 2. Hate
speech--United States. 3. Freedom of speech--United States.
4. College students--Civil rights--United States. I. Title.
II. Series: Symposium series ; v. 44)
LC212.42.N53 1997
378.1'012--dc20   95-49261
                                                              CIP

This is volume 44 in the continuing series
Symposium Series
Volume 2   ISBN 0-7734-8847-2
SS Series ISBN 0-88946-989-X

A CIP catalog record for this book is available from the British Library.

The Edwin Mellen Press   The Edwin Mellen Press
      Box 450   Box 67
Lewiston, New York   Queenston, Ontario
   USA 14092-0450   CANADA L0S 1L0

The Edwin Mellen Press, Ltd.
Lampeter, Dyfed, Wales
UNITED KINGDOM SA48 7DY

Printed in the United States of America

Also by George Anastaplo

Books
The Constitutionalist: Notes on the First Amendment
Human Being and Citizen: Essays on Virtue, Freedom and the Common Good
The Artist as Thinker: From Shakespeare to Joyce
The Constitution of 1787: A Commentary
The American Moralist: On Law, Ethics, and Government
The Amendments to the Constitution: A Commentary
Plato's "Meno": Translation and Commentary (with John Gormly)
The Thinker as Artist: On the Divine from Homer to Raphael

Book-length Law Review Collections
Human Nature and the First Amendment
What is Still Wrong with George Anastaplo? A Sequel to 366 U.S. 82
Church and State: Explorations
Slavery and the Constitution: Explorations
Freedom of Speech and the First Amendment: Explorations
The Constitution at Two Hundred: Explorations
On Trial: Explorations
On Freedom: Explorations
Rome, Piety, and Law: Explorations
*Lessons for the Student of Law: The Oklahoma Lectures**
*Law & Literature and the Bible: Explorations**
*Law & Literature and Shakespeare: Explorations**

*in course of preparation

CONTENTS

PREFACE

A misunderstanding came up one time between Abe Lincoln and William Grigsby. It ended with Grigsby so mad he challenged Abe to a fight. Abe looked down at Grigsby, smiled, and said the fight ought to be with John Johnston, Abe's stepbrother. The day was set for the fight; each man was there with his seconds; the mauling began with the two fighters stripped to the waist, beating and bruising each other with bare knuckles.

A crowd stood around, forming a ring, cheering, yelling, hissing, till after a while, they saw Johnson getting the worst of it. Then the ring of people forming the crowd was broken as Abe Lincoln shouldered his way through, stepped out, took hold of Grigsby and threw that fighter out of the center of the fight-ring.

— Carl Sandburg

The savage bombing of an Oklahoma City federal office building, on April 19, 1995, has dramatized longstanding questions among us about irresponsible talk. Particularly troubling have been the desperate fantasies of those who have long considered the United States subverted by racial and other minorities. Such subversion, it is believed by the xenophobic, makes this country susceptible to the tyranny of worldwide conspiracies.

Perhaps the most dreadful xenophobic campaign anywhere since the Hitler regime in Germany and the Stalinist regimes in Russia and China has been endured in Cambodia. The butchery resorted to there in the 1970s, in an effort to wipe out all traces of foreign influence, exhibited organized madness of a perhaps unprecedented intensity. This was probably even worse, because it was more ideological, than the terrible tribal-war bloodletting in Rwanda last year. Particularly significant, in the merciless Pol Pot campaign against everyone in Cambodia with intellectual pretensions, was the recruitment of the very young as reliable agents of the systematic atrocities that were inflicted upon the Cambodian people. Sadism came to be legitimated and intensified in an effort to stamp out all traces of individualism (that is to say, civilization).

Our own impassioned young are also on exhibit in the vicious talk, or verbal terrorism, against which campus hate-speech codes have been directed in the United States during the past two decades. The physical violence we have been subjected to in this country has, up to now, rarely been witnessed on our campuses. Even so, we are confronted by the problem of what may be done, consistent with our constitutional principles and political habits, to discourage if not even to suppress irresponsible speech on campuses. In these matters, rampant individualism has to defer to a proper sense of community.

People, and especially the young, do have to be reminded from time to time that their words can have serious consequences for which they may be held responsible one way or another. But such reminders do not easily "register" with those who have been allowed to become so misinformed and hence so frightened that they can be frightening. Among the illusions abroad in the land (more so than on campuses) is what various of the "patriots" among us are saying these days about the right of revolution endorsed by the Founders of this country. It is clear both from the language of the Declaration of Independence and from the conduct of the Founders, however, that their right-of-revolution principle looks to the replacement of bad government by good government, not to the elimination of government altogether, the advocacy of which (I argue in my Oklahoma City bombing talk) the Founders would have regarded "as at best an amiable fantasy and as at worst dangerous nonsense." The epigraph for the hate-speech part of this collection, taken from the youth of Abraham Lincoln, reminds us that the principles we rely upon should not be mechanically persevered in wherever it becomes obvious that their proper purposes are not being served.

The four talks collected in Part One of this volume address the current problems posed by campus hate-speech codes. These talks were given in 1991-1992: the first in Lubbock, Texas; the second and the third in Memphis, Tennessee; and the fourth in Chicago, Illinois. Each talk was tailored somewhat to its audience. (The opening note for each talk — Notes 1, 21, 30, and 37 — identifies the occasion for its delivery.) That is, an effort was made by me to challenge the presuppositions, while remaining appropriately respectful of the pieties, of the audience addressed on each occasion. It is recognized thereby that there is much to be said on the various sides of this controversy. In addition, the year-long development of my own thinking on this subject may be followed — and this can be instructive as to the problems inherent in whatever position one may take here. Thus, I return in my fourth talk in Part One to the position taken in the first talk after having been obliged (in my second and third talks) to shift my emphasis in response to questionable doctrines. (The first and fourth talks were in law school settings.) These four hate-speech-codes talks were originally published in my 260-page collection, "On Freedom," in volume 17 of the *Oklahoma City University Law Review* (1992). Revisions have been made, primarily in the notes, to permit these talks to stand alone in this volume. Extended discussions by me of points touched upon in these talks may be found in the material cited in the first thirty-nine notes of this volume.

We can be reminded of the dreadful consequences of hateful speech in the world at large by the three talks collected in Part Two of this volume. These talks were given in Chicago, Illinois in 1993-1995. (The opening note for each talk — Notes 40, 53, and 63 — identifies the occasion for its delivery.) The talks in Part Two discuss, in turn, the fate of the Jews in Southern Europe during the Second World War, the current war in Bosnia, and the recent Oklahoma City bombing. We can see in these three talks what may be said for the cause of civilization in grim circumstances. The origins, or foundations, of civilizations are suggested in Part Three of this volume. Questions and issues about the principles and presuppositions drawn upon in Parts One and Two — moral principles and presuppositions with respect to the soul, nature, and the self — are discussed in the two talks collected in Part Three. These talks were given in Little Switzerland, North Carolina and in Irving, Texas in 1995. The opening note for each talk — Note 66 and Note 79 — identifies the occasion for its delivery.

Vital to the concerns expressed in all nine of these talks is the need to restore the standard of civility by which productive discourse is sustained. A model of such civility was graciously provided by a teacher of mine at the University of Chicago four decades ago, C. Herman Pritchett (1907-1995). It is appropriate, therefore, that this volume be dedicated to his memory.

George Anastaplo

Chicago, Illinois

PART ONE

CAMPUS HATE-SPEECH CODES
AND THE CONSTITUTION

I.

HATE SPEECH AND THE FIRST AMENDMENT[1]

i.

A President of the University of Chicago, a former Dean of the Yale Law
School, liked to say in the 1940s that the law school was one place in a university
where a student might learn to read.[2] Perhaps this is still true a half-century
later.

I presume to add a perhaps related observation: the law school may also
be one place in a university where a student might learn how to behave himself
if he does not already know this when he first shows up. This is so whether or
not the particular law school has a formal code of conduct for its students.

How law students should talk to and about others soon becomes apparent
even to the more undisciplined or impassioned among them. Reminders, such as
the salutary one issued by the dean of this law school last fall, reinforce what
should be generally evident:

> While we all recognize the free speech rights of students, this law school does
> not condone race-based harassment, sex-based harassment, or harassment based

---

[1]   This talk was given at the Texas Tech University School of Law, March 27,
1991. The epigraph for this collection is taken from Carl Sandburg, *Abraham Lincoln: The
Prairie Years* (New York: Harcourt, Brace and Co., 1926), 1: 51.

[2]   That was Robert M. Hutchins. See George Anastaplo, "Remarks on Law &
Literature," *Loyola University of Chicago Law Journal*, 23: 199, 201 (1992). See, on Mr.
Hutchins, Anastaplo, "Freedom of Speech and the First Amendment: Explorations," *Texas Tech
Law Review*, 21: 1941, 2033-40 (1990). See also, John A. Murley, Robert L. Stone, and William
T. Braithwaite, eds., *Law and Philosophy: The Practice of Theory* (Athens, Ohio: Ohio
University Press, 1992), 2: 1097 (Item 13).

> on ethnic origin or religion . . . . The administration of this school will make
> appropriate responses to acts of harassment, including, where appropriate,
> referral to character and fitness committees of state bar organizations.

Thus, students are reminded that their professors are entitled, if not even obliged, to exercise their own freedom of speech in reporting to others what they think of students who carry on in a certain way. No doubt, most students, not only those in law school, realize that they cannot reasonably expect to be liked by their influential professors when they do unseemly things without regard to the interests or sensibilities of others. The discipline imposed upon law students with respect to these matters stands them in good stead when they must deal thereafter with difficult clients, touchy fellow lawyers, and unreasonable judges, however the First Amendment may be interpreted for the community at large.

Hate speech, as it is called these days, is but one form of misconduct for which students may be penalized, informally if not formally. Precisely what the rules should be in these matters very much depends on circumstances, something that is best left for each campus to work out for itself. Even inferior rules are to be preferred to an "ideal" system if those rules are worked out locally by the faculty, students, and administration to whom they apply. No doubt, those who fashion such rules want to draw on models and discussions elsewhere, of which there are now many. No outsider is needed to provide what is readily available without his help. Even so, I have been invited to address the issues involved here — and this I do by suggesting facets of the problem that I have not seen discussed elsewhere in the way I propose to do.

ii.

The critical requirement in these as in most controversial matters is to see and hear things as they truly are. What is needed to accomplish this? It should be determined in the course of any inquiry here what *has* been happening in this country. It is widely said that more hateful things are being said on campuses in this country than ever before. If this is so, why is it happening? Is it because of the way students are being trained before they come to the college campus? This would raise questions about the general mood of the country, including the political leadership that has (or has not) been generally available with respect to such matters. Or is it because of policies and practices that students encounter on campuses? It is sometimes said that some students are reacting with abusive speech to the unfairness they perceive in the affirmative-action programs they encounter on campuses and elsewhere. But it should be noticed that, whatever there may be to this observation, it does not account for the considerable abuse that is reported to have been directed at persons and groups who are clearly *not* the intended beneficiaries of any affirmative-action programs.[3]

Any determination of what in fact is happening today should consider whether the principal shift has been not in the amount of abusive speech but rather in the heightened sensitivity of those who have long, if not always, been the targets of abuse. Perhaps both the abuser and the victim are now less inhibited than before in making their opinions publicly known in these matters. The friction we are hearing about may be one natural consequence of increased contact between groups that had once been more or less isolated from each other.

Among the things that have certainly been happening is the questioning of anti-harassment rules on campuses as "the new McCarthyism," as the current form of mob rule.[4] Such complaints have to be taken seriously, for no rules can

---

[3]   Among those abused considerably by hate speech have been Jews, who are not beneficiaries of any program. See, on affirmative-action programs, Anastaplo, *The American Moralist: On Law, Ethics and Government* (Athens, Ohio: Ohio University Press, 1992), pp. xxii, 473. See, also, Anastaplo, *The Amendments to the Constitution: A Commentary* (Baltimore: Johns Hopkins University Press, 1995), pp. 181-84, 236, 439, 441-42, 452.

[4]   See e.g., Allan Bloom, *The Closing of the American Mind* (New York: Simon and Schuster, 1987); Dinesh D'Souza, *Illiberal Education: The Politics of Race and Sex on Campus* (New York: Free Press, 1991). Compare Robert L. Stone, ed., *Essays on "The Closing*

maintain the respect they need for their effectiveness if they are regarded as suppressive of legitimate freedom of speech. Whether these rules *are* free-speech violations can become secondary, if not even irrelevant, if they should come to be widely regarded to be such. Everyone on campus needs to be able to criticize academic policies, not only affirmative-action and related policies but also the policies about what is condemned as abusive speech. Those who stand for public decency on campus — and that, I take it, is an important objective of those who would curb abusive speech — those who stand for public decency have to take care lest they concede to alleged offenders, or to their well-meaning defenders, high ground from which to attack. All this should remind us that there is in such matters no substitute for prudential judgment.

iii.

High ground *is* vital in these matters. In order to see things properly one must have a higher perspective than is ordinarily available. Only then can one really see things, including what can be done and how — and what can be done rarely, if at all. This permits one to be aware of what the underlying problems are and what the best thinking about them has been over the centuries.

Critical to the recent emergence of uninhibited speech on campus may be the general opinion that has been developing for some time now about "individuality" and "self-expression." It has become fashionable to say that the role of the community in the shaping of the moral and other opinions of a people should be limited if not even eliminated. Things have come to such a pass that some conservatives — who can be rather vigorous these days in their criticisms of anti-harassment policies on campuses — are insisting in effect that the

---

of the American Mind" (Chicago: Chicago Review Press, 1989).

promotion of virtue is no business of the community.[5]

Conservatives have become so exercised about these matters that they have evidently joined forces with the American Civil Liberties Union in attempts to secure Congressional legislation designed to ensure that students attending colleges and universities be able to exercise freedom of speech without fear of academic sanctions.[6] This approach means, in effect, that academic bodies would be governed in these matters by the United States Supreme Court's interpretations of the First and Fourteenth Amendments. Does this also mean, for example, that academic authorities should not be able to prevent or to penalize the burning of the American flag on a campus?[7] Whatever may be said about such immunity in the community at large, do conservatives really want to go this far on campus?

One of the exceptions routinely provided for when this approach is taken

---

[5]   The issue here is not with respect to outside speakers who are sometimes shouted down on campuses, but rather with respect to the conscientious efforts of a school to shape its own students. See Anastaplo, "Freedom of Speech and the First Amendment," 1958. See, also, note 31, below.

[6]   The comment in the text draws upon an early 1991 Senate version of the "Freedom of Speech on Campus Act of 1991" which was introduced later in the year in the House of Representatives. See H. R. Rep. No. 3451, 102nd Cong., 1st Sess. (1991); H. R. Rep. No. 1380, 102nd Cong., 1st Sess. (1991); S. Rep. No. 1484, 102nd Cong., 1st Sess. (1991). See, also, L. Gordon Crovitz, "Henry Hyde and the ACLU Propose a Fate Worse that PCness," *Wall Street Journal*, May 1, 1991, p. A15; Henry J. Hyde and George M. Fishman, "The Collegiate Speech Protection Act of 1991: A Response to the New Intolerance in the Academy," *Wayne Law Review*, 37: 1142, 1165 (1991); Elaine S. Povich, "ACLU Joins Hyde in Free-Speech Fight," *Chicago Tribune*, March 12, 1991, p. 6; Basil Talbot, "Odd Allies Fight Conduct Codes," *Chicago Sun-Times*, March 11, 1991, p. 6. See, as well, note 8, below.

[7]   See, e.g., *Texas* v. *Johnson*, 491 U. S. 397 (1989). See, also, Anastaplo, "Bork on Bork," *Northwestern University Law Review*, 84: 1142, 1165 (1990). A rather frivolous constitutional amendment authorizing anti-flag-desecration laws is being considered in the current Congress.

is that it should not apply to the military academies.[8] In such institutions, it seems, the promotion of community spirit and the shaping of character may be taken more seriously by academic authorities. But if ordinary schools try to promote civility on campus, it also seems, they are to have the Constitution waved at them.[9]

iv.

What is in fact needed depends in part on what has been happening in this country. I have not personally witnessed the sort of harassing conduct complained of. I *have* seen certain slogans, as on publicly-displayed tee-shirts, that can be (at least for those no longer young) like a slap in the face even though they may not be directed at any particular person or group. An imposition by one person upon others can be quite gratuitous and otherwise a considerable surprise. This can give one a notion of what harassing speech of a personal character can be like in its effects, especially when it begins to look like the modern tort of intentional infliction of emotional distress.

If there is much more harassing speech than I have witnessed on campuses, it is probably because offenders are concerned about the effects they have on people other than their targets. That is, much of such conduct seems to be hidden from general view, is done anonymously, or is otherwise concealed.

---

[8]   See, e.g., "Freedom of Speech on Campus Act of 1991," H. R. Rep. No. 3451, 102nd Cong., 1st Sess. (1991):

> [The provisions of the Act] shall not apply to an institution of higher education (A) that is controlled by or affiliated with a religious organization, if the application of this section would not be consistent with the religious tenets of such organization; or (B) whose primary purpose is the training of individuals for (i) the military service of the United States, or (ii) the merchant marine.

[9]   See "Race, Law, and Civilization," in Anastaplo, *Human Being and Citizen: Essays on Virtue, Freedom, and the Common Good* (Chicago: Swallow Press/Ohio University Press, 1975), p. 175. See, also, Shelby Steele, "The Recoloring of Campus Life," *Harper's Magazine*, February 1989, pp. 47, 55.

This also suggests that some offenders know better, that they sense that what they are doing is not regarded as honorable, and that they are not likely to be benefitted either in their immediate safety or in their long-term careers if it is generally known what they are doing. In some ways, many (perhaps most) of the offenders are like the cemetery vandals one hears of from time to time (as in the Chicago area recently): they do not really see what they *are* doing; they do not grasp the enormity of their larks in the eyes of others.

Still, it should again be noticed, things are far better in some respects than when I first found myself on a college campus more than four decades ago. There is now much more of a place on campuses for women and minorities, both of which groups are said to have become targets of more and more abusive speech. Or, as Shelby Steele has put it, "I think racial tension on campus is the result more of racial equality than inequality."[10]

v.

Many offenders, I have suggested, may not see what they truly look like. They would be better able to see things — and would be themselves better seen by others — if artists were to depict them for what they often are: disturbed and hence disturbing people. Art can be important in such matters, for it can make certain things clearer by showing what there *is* to be seen.[11]

What *is* to be seen in the more troublesome hate-speech situations about which we hear? The most obvious thing to be seen is the ugliness, or hatefulness, of various kinds of cruelty. If one does see it clearly, one is likely

---

[10]   Steele, "The Recoloring of Campus Life," p. 48.

[11]   See, on Clovis and his response to the *story* of the Crucifixion, Anastaplo, "On Trial: Explorations," *Loyola University of Chicago Law Journal*, 42: 765 n.763. Consider, also, the Garrison Keillor episode described in Anastaplo, "On Trial," pp. 618-19.

to have a natural aversion to it.[12]   There *is* something seriously wrong with those who indulge themselves in this fashion, although perhaps not as much so when they are young people who have been drinking (as is reported in a few of the more notorious incidents).

There should not be much of an argument about what we want to have. What we want are communities without such hateful talk about, however robust the criticism among us may be of issues and, if need be, of personalities. Among the questions that confront us here are: How is that which we want to be achieved? At what cost? And with what long-term effects? It should at once be added that it may be difficult to define precisely what is objectionable: such assessments, too, depend on prudential judgment, and prudence cannot be subjected to rules.

vi.

It is not prudent to deny that there are ugly things in the world that we are entitled, if not obliged, to recognize for what they are. The proper response to the ugly varies with the circumstances, including one's talents and station. It helps, I have suggested, to survey these matters from high ground. Perhaps the highest ground provided for most of us is supplied by the works of art to which I have referred.

A particularly useful work of art here comes from the playwright, Aeschylus, in Fifth Century Greece. The culmination of his trilogy, the *Oresteia*, deals with the consequences of the matricide which Apollo orders and for which the Furies are pursuing Apollo's agent, Orestes.

Apollo, a god associated with light and beauty, comes upon the primitive

---

[12]   See, on the lessons here of the Nuremberg Trial of 1945-1946, Anastaplo, "On Trial," pp. 977-94. See, also, Anastaplo, *Human Being and Citizen*, pp. 109-10; Anastaplo, "The Fate of the Jews in Greece and Italy During the Second World War," *The Greek Star*, Chicago, Illinois, January/February 1995 (reprinted in Part Two of this Collection).

Furies at his shrine in Delphi where Orestes had fled from them for protection. He speaks to them:

> Out with you! And be quick about it!
> Go, rid the prophetic sanctuary of your presence,
> lest the winged gleaming snake,
> sped by the golden bowstring, overtake you!
>   . . . .
> The whole aspect of your shape is a sure guide.
> You are such things as ought to haunt the cave
> of the blood-gulping lion; you should not rub
> your infection off on a nearby oracle.
> Be gone, unshepherded by any herdsman!
> To such a flock as you, no god feels kindly.

We can see that the ugliness of the Furies repels Apollo mightily. He instinctively strikes out at them. There is something about them that he finds threatening and offensive.

Similarly, in confronting what is called hate speech, it is the *hate*, not the *speech* or even the ideas (insofar as they can be distinguished from the hate), which repels the sensitive.

vii.

We return to the *Oresteia*. Orestes, still under the protection of Apollo, is directed by him to go to Athens where the goddess Athena will judge the dispute between Orestes and the vengeful Furies.

Athena comes to her shrine and finds there both Orestes as supplicant and the fiercesome Furies who pursue him. This is how *she* responds to the scene she confronts:

> Here I see this company,
> new to this land. I am not afraid, but wonder;
> I look and wonder. Who can they be? I speak
> to all of you — to you, and to the stranger [Orestes]
> seated at my image. You there [referring to the Furies],
> who are not like to anything begotten,
> neither among goddesses whom the gods have seen
> nor similar to mortal shape — yet it is wrong

> to speak ill to one that meets you without offense;
> that is not justice nor the sacred law.[13]

Thus Athena, too, is aware of the Furies' ugliness. But, unlike Apollo, she is not simply repelled. Rather, she is intrigued by them and seeks to understand their position. She is not "threatened" by them. Instead, she undertakes to examine their grievances. Similarly, we can hope, academicians can strive to understand the offensive-sounding things that they happen to encounter, things that remind us of Furies that lie submerged in the souls of many if not most human beings.

Athena, it becomes evident in Aeschylus' account, is much better equipped — by temperament and perhaps otherwise — to assess the Furies sensibly. In dealing with the Furies and in getting them to be and to do what she wants, Athena uses both persuasion and threats. We can see here that sanctions are legitimately used in the service of justice (she has access, she pointedly reminds the Furies, to Zeus' thunderbolts). We can also see that the Furies need to be offered something that ministers to their concerns.

Critical to Athena's effectiveness is that she does recognize her superior position.

viii.

Those academicians, including students, who can become quite upset by the hate speech they encounter on campus may not always recognize their superior position. They are indeed superior even if they are the targets and victims of such speech, but they may not be as superior as they could be.

If they only knew how superior they were, they could shrug off (perhaps even laugh off) the attacks directed at them. But they may not be mature enough

---

[13]   The *Eumenides* passages are taken from a translation by David Grene and Wendy Doniger of Aeschylus, *Oresteia* (Chicago: University of Chicago Press, 1989), lines 180-97, pp. 403-13. See, on the *Oresteia*, Anastaplo, "On Trial," pp. 796-821.

to do that. The more mature among us can diagnose such attacks as often symptomatic of the helplessness, if not even the despair, of the attackers.

The failure of the educational system, in their upbringing, may be evident in the misconduct of offenders in these matters. But there may be something of a failure exhibited also in the inability of targeted persons to respond with equanimity to the attacks upon them. Whether the offenders hurt anyone may depend, in large part, on how the targets take it, especially if they have time to reflect upon what is happening.

Some of the targets of such attacks see themselves as "the real people," dismissing their attackers as unworthy of their concern. They cannot take seriously the *talk* of denigration, however many precautions they may have to take against the actions that such talk may incite. Aside from the occasional destructive action that it might provoke, the fact of the matter is that most hate speech cannot have any harmful effects if the intended victims are informed enough, confident enough, and generally in good shape themselves. It is the inadequacies or vulnerabilities in the targets that such speech depends on for much of its effectiveness.

There may be, then, at least as much need to raise up (or educate) the targets of hate speech as there is to restrain (or punish) its perpetrators. The targets are likely to be more accessible to people of good will than are the perpetrators.

ix.

Athena teaches those who confront ugly things how best to respond to them. One needs to be calm and collected, inquiring into what is indeed going on and why.

It will not do for Athena to fail to appreciate why Apollo responds as he does to the terribly ugly Furies that he encounters. Nor will it do for her to fail to appreciate what the offensive Furies truly want. After all, the Furies are like Apollo himself in one critical respect: they are responding, in their crude instinctual way, to an ugliness that *they* see, in this case, the ugliness of matricide, however that matricide came about.

The Furies have become ugly (or, if always ugly, they have become uglier) by having had to respond so much, and for so long, to the ugliness they must deal with. We can be reminded by their fate that one must take care not to allow one's own soul to become twisted by the evil one is obliged to oppose.[14]

There was a need or purpose in what the Furies had long done in their primitive response to certain deeds. For example, they protected against misdeeds hidden inside the home. This kind of protection is something that we can appreciate the need for today as we hear of the abuses concealed within the family circle from the general view and hence from adequate public supervision. Athena, for one, recognizes that the community cannot do completely without the crude responses associated with the Furies.

x.

These are lessons suggested by Aeschylus that we can bring to our assessment of the hate-speech phenomenon on campuses. Relevant lessons are available as well from teachers such as Plato and Aristotle, especially their insistence that all actions aim at some good.[15] This insistence makes us suspect that it must be rare to have a prejudice without there being something upon which it is somehow based.

---

[14]   This is a risk that career prosecutors have to guard against. Compare the English system which can find a barrister routinely prosecuting and defending in criminal cases, depending on the briefs he receives from day to day.

[15]   See, e.g., Plato, *Republic* 517B-C; Aristotle, *Nicomachean Ethics* (beginning); Aristotle, *Politics* (beginning).

Although there may be something atavistic about our prejudices (as there is about the Furies), there is also likely to be something defensible about them. The "different" is in itself a problem: it challenges one's own, which can be bothersome when one believes that one's own has been doing fairly well but is now vulnerable because of changing circumstances.

Prejudices, then, should be examined — if Athena's approach is to be followed — in order to discover the element of truth or justice that may be concealed within them. The offender, like the intended victim and the authorities, must be given his due if the situation is to be fully understood and most effectively dealt with. His needs and concerns must be addressed one way or another.

xi.

I recapitulate: Hate speech, or the prejudices it expresses, reflects one or more sets of failings. It may be partly due to the failings, including the damaged soul, of the offender. (These are, of course, the most obvious shortcomings.) It may be partly due also to the failings of the community in dealing with inequities and in shaping citizens. (This may be seen in some of the resentment at affirmative-action programs.) It may be partly due as well to the failings of the victims themselves. (This may be seen in a victim's tendency to supply the role of victim or to respond in such a way as to encourage attack by the callous or vicious.)

Victims *are* often different enough to be noticed. Sometimes the victims can even appear inferior in the way they live and in how they look. Sometimes, of course, that obvious difference may reflect a superior way of life, but it may not be generally recognized as such. That which is disparaged as laziness, for example, may be really be a form of freedom.[16] Consider how Socrates, who could be condemned as shiftless by many if not most Athenians, is generally regarded by us. What the Athenians did not recognize were the ways in which Socrates was decisively superior to them. Their democratic presuppositions may have discouraged them from facing up to the truth of the matter.

Our own democratic presuppositions, including our dedication to the proposition that all men are created equal, may contribute both to the recourse by some to hate speech and to the fervent opposition by others to it. Much of our hate speech these days implicitly challenges a routine dedication to equality in that it points to what the offensive speaker considers natural differences between male and female or between races or peoples that it has become generally unfashionable, if not even dangerous, to notice and acknowledge.

That there are significant natural differences between human beings can be hard to deny. This is most obvious to us when we see superb athletes performing. One critical problem we have here, however, is how we can recognize the role of nature in these matters without seeming to endorse or legitimate prejudices that trick themselves out as "natural."

xii.

It is partly because the victims, or their would-be benefactors, may be somewhat at fault themselves that the freedom of speech issue comes up when attempts are made to regulate hate speech on campus. There may indeed be things done by or for the victims that should be exposed to public criticism.

Also, it is tempting to dismiss as mere prejudice what may be honest reporting or conscientious opposition. To attack critics as prejudiced may be a

---

[16]   This is something that Americans may come to appreciate if they should continue to be disparaged by the Japanese for "laziness." See e.g., Anastaplo, *The American Moralist*, p. 447. A remarkable yearning for freedom helps account for various, sometimes questionable and sometimes attractive, features of the European Gypsies that I have studied.

way of concealing the truth of a matter. It is well, when confronting such "prejudiced" critics, to see what it is that troubles them, which may be in some (but not all) cases the condition of their own souls.

We should not want, in any event, to punish or silence unpopular challenges to accepted opinions. The underprivileged in a community are not usually helped in an atmosphere of suppression. Suppression, after all, is usually controlled by the privileged. It should, therefore, usually be discouraged as a proper response to opinions condemned as offensive.

xiii.

I should not leave these closing comments about the First Amendment problem in dealing with hate speech without observing that the more offensive conduct here is usually *not* entitled to "freedom of speech" protection. It should at once be added, however, that the hate speaker is still left with substantial protection even if the mantle of "freedom of speech" is removed from him. Due process considerations are vital here as are prudential assessments of the responses to and consequences of what is done to suppress hate speech.

The freedom-of-speech arguments we have been hearing depend, in large part, on the current tendency to substitute the term *freedom of expression* for the more rigorous constitutional language, *freedom of speech, or of the press.* Freedom of speech as it developed in the Anglo-American constitutional system goes back to the parliamentary privilege: it was intended to protect those who undertook to discuss the public business; it was not intended to protect or license self-expression. The parliamentary privilege was consistent with the respect required for decorum in the forum where the protected discussion took place.[17]

---

[17]   See, e.g., Anastaplo, *The Constitutionalist: Notes on the First Amendment* (Dallas: Southern Methodist University Press, 1971), pp. 239-53. See, also, note 24, below. See, on decorum, Talk IV of Part Two, below.

This decorum, which was considered essential to the most productive examination of issues, is comparable to the civility needed on campus if an educational institution is to be able to accomplish its proper missions.

Those who do not exhibit conventional civility can be expected to suffer at the hands of others in a variety of ways. People who abuse others should not be surprised if there is a hostile, even hateful, response to them when they are detected.[18] One way or another, for example, the immature people who parade offensive slogans (just like the people who burn flags) will be penalized by the community at large, if only by being despised and shunned. (Thus, tolerated "hate speech" can run in two directions.)

To speak of decorum here is to be reminded of the place of the community, and of natural right, in shaping and guiding us all. It can affect adversely the tone of the community if all efforts on behalf of civility should be dismissed as attempts to suppress free speech. I yield to no one in my reservations about the wisdom of what we have done since last November in the Persian Gulf. But a community with a self-confidence that is grounded in common sense would not permit the "day-and-night drumbeat of antiwar demonstrators camped out in Lafayette Park across Pennsylvania Avenue" from the White House. No citizen — and that should include the President of the United States who is said to be weary because the drums keep him up much of the night — should be subjected to such abuse in the name of freedom of speech.[19]

---

[18]   This is related to the "fighting words" exception in the law of the First Amendment. See Harry Kalven, Jr., *A Worthy Tradition: Freedom of Speech in America* (New York: Harper & Row, 1988), pp. 16-19, 78-95, 110-16.

[19]   See Evan Thomas and Ann McDaniel, "Bush's United Front," *Newsweek*, March 4, 1991, p. 49. See, on the Gulf War, Anastaplo, "On Freedom: Explorations," *Oklahoma City University Law Review*, 17: 465, 589-630. See, on the Vietnam War, Anastaplo, *The American*

It is a mistake, then, to make much of the constitutional or legal issues in assessing what should be done about hate speech on American campuses. It is much more a human, a prudential, a political issue. It is also a mistake for lawyers and for teachers of lawyers to place the emphasis, in explaining how the law works, upon "teeth" or sanctions. Rather, the law tends to teach us what is right and wrong: we generally prefer to do what we have come to believe *is* right, whether or not it is likely that we will be penalized for acting otherwise.[20]

In various ways, therefore, the community must indicate what it considers good. This depends, in part, on its confidence both in its own ability to distinguish good from bad and in its right to do something about what it does know about both good and bad. A properly constituted community can effectively *teach* one and all that the most serious consequence of indulging oneself in certain unseemly passions and opinions is *not* what might be done by the authorities if one happens to be caught. Rather, the most serious consequence of such self-indulgence is that one escapes detection and correction, thereby being condemned to be ever after the kind of person who thinks and says things unworthy of a civilized human being.

Moralist, pp. 225-44.

[20]   See, e.g., Anastaplo, *The American Moralist*, p. 375. See, on how lawyers should conduct themselves, Anastaplo, "On Crime, Criminal Lawyers, and O. J. Simpson: Plato's *Gorgias* Revisited," *Loyola University of Chicago Law Review*, 26: 455 (1995); Anastaplo, "Lessons for the Student of Law," *Oklahoma City University Law Review*, 19: 1 (1995). See, also, Anastaplo, "Natural Law or Natural Right?," *Loyola University of New Orleans Law Review*, 38: 915 (1993); Murley, Stone, and Braithwaite, eds., *Law and Philosophy*, 1: 413-538. See, on C. Herman Pritchett (to whom this collection of talks on campus hate-speech codes and Twentieth Century atrocities is dedicated), *ibid.*, 1: 539.

II.

HATE SPEECH, CIVILITY, AND EDUCATION[21]

i.

Stanley Fish is correct to notice that there are presuppositions and purposes in any legal and constitutional system that may be relied upon by a community.[22] The rules of the system are likely to reflect those presuppositions and purposes: it is not merely a game that is being played without reference to anything outside it.

When things break down, the usual rules may have to be set aside. Such setting aside may be seen in the provision in the Constitution of 1787 for suspending the privilege of the writ of *habeas corpus* in prescribed circumstances. Such setting aside may also be seen in what President Lincoln was obliged to do, outside of the Constitution, in the face of a threatened disintegration of the Union. [This can even be said to have been anticipated, in spirit, by the "sovereign" intervention by Abraham Lincoln in the episode recorded in the epigraph to this Collection.]

ii.

Considerations of this character seem to lead Professor Fish to justify, if

---

[21]   This talk was given to the Gilliland Symposium, Rhodes College, Memphis, Tennessee, October 30, 1991. Stanley Fish, of Duke University, was the other speaker on that occasion. See note 30, below. See, on Stanley Fish, Adam Begley, "Souped-up Scholar," *New York Times Magazine*, May 3, 1992, p. 38.

[22]   See Stanley Fish, "There's No Such Thing as Free Speech and It's a Good Thing Too," *Boston Review*, February 1992, p. 3. See, on what a free and responsible press can look like, Andrew Patner, *I. F. Stone: A Portrait* (New York: Pantheon Books, 1988). See, also, Richard M. Weaver, *Ideas Have Consequences* (Chicago: University of Chicago Press, 1948).

not also to emphasize, certain restraints these days upon what may be said on campuses. He argues, in effect, that particular prohibitions may be laid down in the interest of preserving the system upon which the academic community relies. These prohibitions, with respect to what may be said about racial, gender, sexual, and religious differences, can be understood to promote civility on campus and to permit thereby the disciplined discourse necessary for meaningful education.

The widespread attractiveness of what Mr. Fish advocates these days is testified to by the recent recourse on a number of campuses to "speech codes." But, I presume to suggest, the case made here by him and by others of like mind may go too far and yet not go far enough.

iii.

It can be difficult to argue in sensitive times that speech codes may go too far in protecting, say, racial minorities from scurrilous attacks by their fellow students and others on campus, but we must try.

We, including those among us who are members of harassed minorities, need to hear more about what prejudiced people believe and why. Such deeply flawed opinions *are* out there and have to be reckoned with. They do not go away or are not likely to be lessened in intensity when they are driven underground, especially when they are fed by resentments at what are believed to be injustices such as "racial quotas" or "reverse discrimination," if not even by real or imagined defects among the people who are attacked.

Members of minorities, as well as their friends, have to become accustomed to dealing with abusive speech. Whatever may be done about it on campuses, abuse remains virulent in the everyday world. The targets of abuse should be able, with the help of their defenders, to deal with much that is said on campus without directly suppressing it.

The further such abusive talk is from a straightforward discussion of ideas, the more susceptible it is likely to be to some regulation. If the abusive speech takes the form of physical threats, it invites (perhaps requires) intervention by the authorities. The same might be said about mere epithets as well as about anonymous scurrility.

One safeguard in the recourse to any regulation is that the official efforts be evenhanded. For example, the discouragement of labelling certain unpopular opinions as *communist* should be matched by the discouragement of labelling still other unpopular opinions as *fascist*. If evenhandedness is not evident to everyone, a particular political agenda on the part of the regulators can be suspected. If evenhandedness is not insisted upon, "power plays" (or mere acts of will) can be expected from ambitious people — and to such forms of domination a principled resistance can be expected.

The precautions I have been sketching mean, in effect, that formal regulations even of offensive speech should be kept to a minimum on campuses. But it should be recognized that informal restraints are many. For example, those who resent and oppose the abusive speakers have at least as much "right" as do such speakers to voice their own sentiments — and to adjust accordingly their relations with the abusive speakers. The abusive speakers, when exposed to public view, can come to see that they are not helping themselves or their careers by conducting themselves as they do.

One way or another, therefore, people on campuses should be taught how to talk civilly to and about each other — and with a minimum of formal suppression of unfortunate speech.

iv.

The defense, if not advocacy, of suppression may go too far also if it should dramatize the *danger* of certain abusive utterances. Talk of "danger" bolstered, if it did not lead to, the notorious "clear and present danger" test devised at the end of the First World War for dealing with supposed threats to the safety of the United States.[23]

This approach, which has had dire effects on freedom of speech in the United States for decades, justifies in the public mind suppression of unpopular political positions because that which threatens any popular position is easily condemned as dangerous. This contributed to the wasteful folly of the Cold War since the Second World War.

There *are* risks to be run when freedom is exercised among a people. "Freedom of speech" is not much of an issue if there is not some speech which is troublesome and even dangerous and which the authorities (if not also the people at large) would prefer not to have had uttered or to have heard.

Critical here is the political context and purpose of our traditional freedom of speech.[24]   The widespread substitution in recent decades of the now fashionable term *freedom of expression* for the traditional term *freedom of speech and of the press* conceals the primary political purpose of the right being invoked here.

If we better apprehend the political purposes of freedom of speech, we can more willingly put up with its risks.   It is far easier to justify "hearing everything" (including unpopular, even inflammatory, things) in order to be able to choose and to act in our true interest as a community than it is to justify "hearing everything" in order to permit people to gratify themselves in the way they happen to please, no matter what the corrupting or disruptive effects on

---

[23]   See *Schenck* v. *United States*, 249 U. S. 47 (1919). See, also, Kalven, *A Worthy Tradition*, p. 179; Alexander Meiklejohn, *Political Freedom: The Constitutional Powers of the People* (New York: Harper Brothers, 1960), pp. 29-50; Anastaplo, *The Constitutionalist*, p. 294.

[24]   Consider how Thomas More, as Speaker of the House of Commons, put this in his address of 1521 to the King. See Anastaplo, *The Amendments to the Constitution*, pp. 256-58. See, also, note 17, above.

others happen to be. The traditional approach to the First Amendment, therefore, calls for virtually unlimited political discourse even as it permits regulations of obscenity, advertising, and other forms of commercial or self-gratifying expression. Such regulations are themselves restrained, of course, by due process and other safeguards.

With these remarks we can now move from a sketch of the argument that the case for campus-speech codes may go too far to a sketch of the argument that that case may not go far enough.

v.

We have already noticed that the case we are examining may not go far enough if it should not be evenhanded in its restrictions — if, for example, it should be highly selective in the forms of scurrility it attempts to suppress. A proper academic community, I have suggested, will try to curtail (preferably by persuasion and example) all forms of incivility.

But incivility is only the tip of the problem that is submerged here. The general acceptance (and not only by Professor Fish) of the term *freedom of expression* tends to license all kinds of talk in our midst, something that makes it difficult for our community to shape properly the character of our people. This openness means, among other things, unlimited scope for commercial pornography and public tastelessness and hence a general coarsening of the public mind and of public sensibilities.

The underlying problem here may be seen in what progressive thinkers (among whom Professor Fish may want to include himself) have in common with some leading conservatives today: the very notion of *corruption* tends to be denied, either intellectual or moral corruption, and especially as something that the community can take notice of and do something about. Thus, conservatives can sometimes make much of the right to choose — a right intimately associated with individuality and the character of private property — but it is difficult (if not impossible) truly to choose if one is either woefully uninformed or deeply corrupted.

It has long been believed by responsible statesmen that there are expressions as well as deeds that should be restrained if the human soul is to be given an opportunity to mature and if human decency is to prevail. All too many among us these days are reluctant to go far enough in providing such wide-ranging restraints (whether formal or informal), settling instead for attempts at suppressing occasional utterances of a particularly scurrilous character by souls that have been allowed to become disturbed.

vi.

It is a mistake, however, to emphasize in these matters what should be (and is not being) suppressed, even though the struggles here do tend to be more dramatic and can easily dominate the scene. So dramatic are they that we lose sight of what needs to be done by way of education (as well as, perhaps, by way of religious training) for the proper shaping of the American people.

Standards have to be insisted upon and developed, and to this end much more than regulations and suppression have to be looked to. This means a pervasive recognition and furtherance of what is most serious.

All this bears on the question, in which there seems to be some interest today, about what the canon of texts should be in our schools, and particularly whether that canon should continue to depend as much as it long has upon the greatest books of the Western world. It is very difficult, perhaps impossible, for the American community at large (and this includes the typical college student) to get much from non-Western classics, however useful it may be to become somewhat familiar with them.[25]

The great conversation from which we can learn what we need to know and to "feel" if we are to be sensible and hence happy human beings — that conversation takes place among the finest minds in the West, minds such as (to mention a few I myself have been privileged to study and write about) the incomparable Jane Austen, the ancient Sappho, the medieval Catherine of Siena, and the modern Virginia Woolf.[26]

vii.

Professor Fish has been fortunate (if I may be permitted to say so) to have worked long and hard on the works of John Milton, earning thereby a considerable reputation for himself in English studies. Even so, I venture to offer a qualification with respect to what he has just said about Milton's *Areopagitica.*[27]

Milton, in his argument for the liberty of the press, does seem to deny to Roman Catholics the privilege of unlicensed printing that he so eloquently advocates. But however prudent it may be to notice such reservations on the part of a partisan thinker, it may be imprudent to make as much of them as Professor Fish does. The implications of a principle can go far beyond what the immediate

---

[25] Thus, I have prepared, for the Encyclopedia Britannica's annual volumes of *Great Ideas Today*, introductions to Confucian Thought (1984), Hindu Thought (1985), Mesopotamian Thought (1986), Islamic Thought (1989), Buddhist Thought (1992), North American Indian Thought (1993), and African Thought (1995).

[26] See, e.g., Anastaplo, *The Artist as Thinker: From Shakespeare to Joyce* (Athens, Ohio: Ohio University Press, 1983), pp. 86-99.

[27] See Fish, "There's No Such Thing as Free Speech," 3-4. See, for his Milton studies, Fish, *Surprised by Sin: The Reader in Paradise Lost* (Berkeley: University of California Press, 1967). See, on Professor Fish's jurisprudence, Sotirios A. Barber, "Stanley Fish and the Future of Pragmatism in Legal Theory," *University of Chicago Law Review*, 58: 1033 (1991). See, on Milton, Anastaplo, *The Artist as Thinker*, pp. 62-74.

framers of that principle were either able to recognize or willing to put up with. This can be said not only about the *Areopagitica*, but also about such other great statements of principle in the Anglo-American heritage as Magna Carta, the Declaration of Independence, and the Fourteenth Amendment.[28]

The implications of a public document are more apt to become fully apparent, or to take hold, when the immediate circumstances of its promulgation are left behind and people finally come to maturity who have been shaped all their lives by the principles implicit in that document. It can also help if those people have moved as a community, partly because of a founding document, beyond the immediate circumstances, interests, and limitations of the framers of that document. Thus, the barons who forced Magna Carta upon King John at Runnymede invoked principles that eventually became difficult for their descendants to deny to the commoners who stood somewhat in the same relation to the barons that the barons stood in relation to the king. The rule of law, if it is truly law, does tend to promote evenhandedness, especially if there is a genuine freedom of speech which permits the doings and sayings of those in authority to be examined and challenged without risk of official sanction.

Among those in authority in this country are the many dedicated women and men who have been entrusted with the education and training of the young from kindergarten through graduate school. Such dedicated teachers should be encouraged to recognize and promote the things that are vital both to the full development of the human soul and to the sustenance of a decent regime.

It has long been believed — and this belief we are entitled and perhaps even obliged to examine in order better to understand things — that there *are*

---

[28]   See Anastaplo, *The Constitution of 1787: A Commentary* (Baltimore: Johns Hopkins University Press, 1989), pp. 6-9; Anastaplo, *The Amendments to the Constitution*, pp. 23-24.

enduring standards, or at least that there are enduring questions that the thoughtful human being should take seriously.

A proper education helps us to recognize and refine the enduring questions as well as to begin to answer them — and to answer them with an awareness of what there may be in the very nature of things that distinguishes attractive falsehoods from the often elusive if not even sometimes bitter truth.[29]

---

[29]   An interview of Professor Fish in the Rhodes College student newspaper quotes him as saying, "[I]n response to my paper, generally what Dr. Anastaplo did was rehearse those very same pieties that I was putting on the table for critical examination. Rather than respond to my analyses of those pieties, he merely repeated them." Stanley Fish Interview, *The Sou'wester*, Nov. 7, 1991, p. 5. See, also, notes 33 and 39, below.

III.

A "HATE SPEECH" ENCOUNTER[30]

i.

We have seen once again, upon being exposed to Stanley Fish's condemnation of "hate speech" last night, how instructive it can be to *have* to tolerate hateful speech. Such speech *can* be disturbing and otherwise unsettling. But it also can help one — especially when such disturbing arguments as Professor Fish's are properly assessed and understood — to get to know oneself better as well as to see better what there may be that should be reckoned with in the opinions of others.[31]

Much of what Professor Fish has to say these days about "freedom of speech" depends, it seems to me, on a disparagement (perhaps even a deliberately provocative disparagement) of the great terms of our tradition, terms such as

---

[30]   This talk was given to the Gilliland Symposium, Rhodes College, Memphis, Tennessee, October 31, 1991. Professor Stanley Fish, of Duke University, met separately with another group at the same time. Both of our groups had heard our talks of the night before. See, note 21, above. See, also, note 33, below.

[31]   In response to an interviewer's suggestion that I had thought that Professor Fish did not have any respect for anyone whose ideas were different from his, he replied,

> Dr. Anastaplo was probably objecting to the fact that I was
> passionate. Liberalism hates passion . . . . I cite David Duke
> as a general piece of evidence. It seems to me that giving to
> certain ideas or policies [a] platform is in fact always going to
> work to the advantage of those ideas[] . . . [s]o that the David
> Duke-Nazi policy is now, I predict, probably going to win the
> governorship of Louisiana. You've got to think about that.
> Don't rest so easily in liberal pieties.

Stanley Fish Interview, p. 5. See, also, note 5, above, note 39, below. Two weeks later Edwin Edwards won what the *New York Times* called a "resounding victory" over David Duke in Louisiana's gubernatorial runoff election.

fairness, *truth*, and *freedom*.[32]   Philosophy is disparaged as altogether
impractical and hence as fit only for the academy, even though it is also only in
the academy that there is permitted the tenor as well as the form of such dismissal
of philosophy as Professor Fish himself indulges in. His kind of talk exhibits
what an argument made almost for its own sake means and leads to. The
possibility of meaningful discourse is subverted thereby. These are hardly lessons
to be taught to youngsters who are prone to be temporarily dazzled by the
pyrotechnics of celebrities who cater to youthful restlessness. Also catered to
here is the iconoclasm of all-too-many intellectuals. (It is one thing to be
skeptical of the icons of one's day — that can be helpful, if pursued in the proper
spirit. It is quite another thing to make an icon of a skepticism that leads to
profound disillusionment.)

Youngsters *can* be dazzled by all this because it seems to offer, especially
to the daring, ready access to power and success. This was the appeal of the
ancient sophists, who were early hit-and-run drivers. Much of what those
intellectuals said, as they moved from one city to another, was for immediate
effect; they were not truly serious thinkers. Or, to adapt to our immediate
purposes an old expression, deep down they were shallow.

ii.

The primary objective of such talk as we have heard from Professor Fish
seems to be *domination*. He probably would not challenge this proposition, but
rather would add that all but the most trivial talk is aimed primarily at
domination. If one is honest with oneself, he has told us, one recognizes that one

---

[32]   See, note 22, above.   See, on irresponsible provocativeness by the
philosophically-minded, Anastaplo, "On Freedom," pp. 683-85.

wants to get one's way, indeed even to silence someone else.[33] The exercise of one's will is made much of by him; the search for truth is systematically disparaged. One can be reminded by all this of the emphasis upon self-assertion found in Martin Heidegger.[34] One is encouraged to become the master not only of all that one surveys, but also of all that one draws upon, including the very language one uses. One thus becomes so dominant as to be able to master all tradition and to subvert all accepted principles.[35] A scholar of reputation who proceeds in this fashion may appear to be taking charge. But such "taking charge" can be a form of suicide instead, and not only because it repudiates what *culture* means and hence whatever may have once guided one's life as a conscientious scholar. An abyss opens up before such a reckless scholar.

It can be instructive to consider the ends to which all that Mr. Fish is now saying is directed. One cannot preach against campus hate speech, as Mr. Fish does these days, without invoking justice, if only tacitly. Some notions of the good must justify and guide the actions that he advocates, a few of which notions can be salutary. One sees in Mr. Fish's approach, however, what the modern

---

[33]   Professor Fish has argued, in the manner of *Thrasymachus* in Plato's *Republic*,
         [P]eople cling to First Amendment pieties because they do not
         wish to face what they correctly take to be the alternative.
         That alternative is *politics*, the realization . . . that decisions
         about what is and is not protected in the realm of expression
         will rest not on principle or firm doctrine, but on the ability
         of some persons to interpret . . . principle and doctrine in
         ways that lead to the protection of speech they want heard and
         the regulation of speech they want silenced.
Fish, "There's No Such Thing as Free Speech," p. 25. See note 31, above, note 39, below.

[34]   Consider, for example, Heidegger's notorious Rektor's Speech in the service of the Nazi regime in 1933. See Anastaplo, *The American Moralist*, pp. 144-60.

[35]   Compare George Orwell's warnings against the debasement of language. See Anastaplo, *The American Moralist*, pp. 161-80.

dethronement of *nature* can lead to.[36]   Nihilism seems critical to the self-centeredness that Mr. Fish both advocates and exhibits. The nihilist needs the ministrations of a thoughtful friend, someone who happens to care for him despite his threats and destructiveness. To recognize that there is something profoundly sad about the aggressive nihilist does not mean that he should not be firmly resisted by men and women of good will who chance to encounter him.

Critical to proper inquiry and to genuine understanding is the condition of one's soul. However influential the Fish rhetoric may be in some quarters, it is ultimately self-defeating. This is partly because decent people instinctively resist this kind of assault, even if they cannot sort out the arguments by which they are being inundated: they sense the unhealthiness of such an approach to human relations; its perversity is apparent to them. One might wonder about the psychic forces that lead to, or that feed, such a condition — but one becomes resigned to the fact that the workings here as elsewhere of history and accident can be mysterious.

iii.

One serious risk of the Fish approach, which explicitly despises liberalism and deliberately ridicules freedom of speech, is that it can undermine the general faith in standards and principles that do restrain (perhaps even inspire) the community at large. Those who indulge themselves in this destructive approach do not seem to appreciate the chance influences that have contributed to the development of tolerant and humane peoples. Mr. Fish and his aggressive coterie, who can inspire vigorous antipathy in their much more conventional fellow citizens, must themselves rely upon the toleration which the community has been trained to respect, the very toleration that Mr. Fish dismisses as

---

[36]   See, e.g., *ibid.*, pp. 412-15. See, also, note 20, above, note 39, below.

inconsequential, if not even as unprincipled and hypocritical.

But he and those of like mind are not the only ones left vulnerable to suppression if the general faith in freedom of speech is subverted in the United States by irresponsible intellectuals. Among the other victims of a general repression would be the very men and women who are moved to do the repressing, which can be ugly both in its manifestations and in its consequences for everyone involved. Those who have experienced tyranny in other lands know how good it is to be free. They know as well that some abuses of any general freedom have to be expected and resisted — and that there are better and worse ways both of heading off abuses and of putting up with the abuses that cannot be headed off.

One must take care, in any event, not to display hate in one's polemics against hate speech. Such polemical attacks sometimes condemn sincere invocations of toleration, truth and fairness as nothing but masks for repression and exploitation. Nor is the "realist's" insistent endorsement of intellectual domination edifying. What we see in such exhibitions of uninhibited self-expression should caution us against unrelenting partisanship and its determination to "win" at all costs. To emphasize that serious speech aims primarily at silencing others is to disparage genuine attempts to pursue inquiries as part of a lifelong effort to learn the truth. A comprehensive disparagement of truth and fairness is all too often grounded in self-hate — in hatred of the best around (and hence in) us. When we happen to observe this warlike phenomenon close-up, we are put on notice about the dark elements that may be lurking in our own souls. We are thus better equipped both to know ourselves and to moderate our own passions, however limited we may be in ministering to the disturbed intellectuals around us who are desperately in need of help. In short, self-hate may be the form of "hate speech" that we in the academy should probably be most concerned about in our present circumstances.

IV.

CAMPUS HATE SPEECH AND A SENSE OF DECORUM[37]

i.

A discussion in the *Washington Post* this past week is entitled "Legislating Thought Crimes." That article, by a respected First Amendment champion, begins:

> In 15th century England, Thomas Burdett literally lost his head because he had committed a crime of thought. On hearing that Edward IV had dispatched a popular white buck with an arrow, Burdett said [that] "he wished the animal, horns and all, were in the king's belly."
>
> It was just a thought, but the law punished the wish. Now, in an increasing number of states, hate crimes — also known as ethnic intimidation statutes — are on the books. They too involve thought crimes — in connection with an act.[38]

We are particularly concerned on this occasion with efforts made on campuses to monitor the kind of aggressive verbal activity associated with "hate crimes."

However troublesome such repressive measures may be — whether they are directed at someone such as Thomas Burdett in Fifteenth Century England or at someone such as a passionate college student in Twentieth Century America — it can be misleading to speak here of "thought crimes." People in these

---

[37]   This talk was given at the Phi Beta Kappa Forum, Northwestern University School of Law, Chicago, Illinois, May 1, 1992.

[38]   Nat Hentoff, "Legislating Thought Crimes," *Washington Post*, April 25, 1992, p. A27.

circumstances are *not* punished for their thoughts alone (whether or not they "believe" the things they happen to say). In the typical case one is punished for one's evident hostility or (more likely) for one's foolishness in expressing one's hostility or for both hostility and foolishness.

Is it not to be expected that one should exercise some judgment with respect to what one does say? Would we have it otherwise? Do we want people to be ignorant of or to disregard natural cause-and-effect connections in human affairs?

ii.

There *are* things one can say that are apt to arouse opposition, sometimes fierce opposition, in others, perhaps even in the community at large. It is usually not difficult for anyone of normal intelligence and sensitivity to figure out, or if need be to learn from painful experience, what the remarks are that are likely to arouse opposition. Two principal kinds of remarks immediately concern us here. They may be conveniently identified as the controversial and the offensive.

Controversial remarks are those that arouse opposition primarily because of *the substance of the arguments* they make or imply. It need not matter precisely where, when, or how they are said. People are apt to be troubled by remarks that question the accepted order, if only by challenging vital opinions of the moment. We may have here speech that can be condemned as sedition or even treason.

Offensive remarks, on the other hand, are those that arouse opposition primarily because of *the way they are put*. It can very much matter here where, when, or how something may be said. The substance of the remarks can be secondary to the way they are conveyed, which can strike various recipients (and not only the intended victims) of the remarks as crude, ugly, perhaps even cruel. We may have here that which can be condemned as malicious incivility and even verbal assault (or the intentional infliction of emotional distress).

Sometimes the controversial and the offensive are combined in the same speech, or are believed to be combined. They *can* be difficult to distinguish in practice. A talk on hate-speech codes, for example, is likely to be controversial these days, no matter what position one takes — and is also likely to seem, if not be, offensive to some. But for our immediate purposes, it is instructive to separate the controversial from the offensive. In these matters a little common sense can go a long way. One useful way of further distinguishing them is to notice that whether or how someone resorts to controversial speech may depend primarily on the virtue of courage and that whether or how someone resorts to offensive speech may depend primarily on the virtue of temperance. In both kinds of situations the virtues of justice and prudence may also be involved.

iii.

By and large, offensive speech should be routinely discouraged among us, if not actually suppressed. Such speech is likely to undermine the social order; or at least it sullies the community, compromising the general pursuit of happiness. Controversial speech, on the other hand, should be, if not encouraged, at least permitted. Such speech stands as a challenge to the policies and practices that we as a community happen to support for the sake of the common good.

Controversial speech is what we have traditionally tried to protect with "freedom of speech" guarantees, as in the 1791 Bill of Rights. Such speech is widely believed to contribute to our ability to assess contending policies and personalities and to make sensible decisions on behalf of the common good.

Offensive speech is what some are currently trying to protect with "freedom of expression" guarantees. The scope of such guarantees may be seen in the wider and wider latitude now permitted to pornography among us. It should be evident from what I say further on in these remarks that "freedom of expression" includes much more than was originally intended by the "freedom of speech" protection found in such places as the First Amendment. Uninhibited freedom of expression, more and more people are coming to believe, contributes to our mental (if not even spiritual) health, to our sense of liberty and well-being, and hence to our personal self-fulfillment. There is, I am afraid, something reckless in this kind of hopefulness at a time when the cause of and experimentation with individuality often take precedence over the needs and claims of the community.

On the other hand, however troublesome (and even dangerously provocative) controversial speech may at times seem and indeed be, a self-governing community such as our learns to live with it. This is, we long ago discovered, what political freedom and effective self-government depend upon.

Efforts *are* made from time to time among us to restrict or to penalize controversial speech, either directly or indirectly — and it is against such restriction that constitutional safeguards are provided. Unofficial measures (which constitutional safeguards can do little about) are also brought to bear upon controversial speech, including frowns, explicit criticisms, and social sanctions.

iv.

Our responses to offensive speech are and should be more complicated than our responses to controversial speech. Offensiveness, which includes disturbing lapses in good taste, is usually monitored routinely, and effectively, by a healthy community. Youngsters, for example, should soon learn what does not help one get along. One does discover in growing up the price one pays for certain kinds of self-indulgence, especially when one depends (as, say, in law school) upon the goodwill of one's teachers and sponsors.

In the light of these observations certain bizarre doings these days at

Harvard Law School testify, in even so privileged a place, to the breakdown of ordinary mutual respect and social restraint, with the faculty ultimately responsible for the painful debacle there.[39] In other circumstances, the size of our associations may tempt the most disturbed elements among us to believe that they can strike out at others anonymously, especially if social guidance no longer suffices to rein us all in. This is likely to be the case in our larger schools, just as it is (in a far grimmer form) in the serial killers who occasionally go on rampages in our cities. A general breakdown in civility is thus threatened on campus, often reflecting underlying causes of discontent and misapprehensions. If the breakdown in civility on campus takes the form either of systematic harassment or of incitement to violence, it can usually be handled in a generally satisfactory manner by academic authorities. But what if it takes the form "only" of such manifestations as pervasive meanspiritedness and massive ugliness? Consider also the concern that people on campus may have about the violence to which the targets of offensive speech may resort in retaliation to systematic insults. The post-Rodney King-trial eruptions in Los Angeles this week should remind us of suppressed rage that can be looking for an "excuse" to vent itself.

A breakdown in civility, however troublesome and even destructive in itself, is also a threat to that productive political discussion which is the primary

---

[39] See, on the sophomoric mocking of a female law professor who had been killed in the Boston area, Abigail Thernstrom, "The Vile Circus at Harvard Law," *Wall Street Journal*, May 1, 1992, p. A14; Fox Butterfield, "Parody Puts Harvard Law Faculty in Sexism Battle," *New York Times*, April 27, 1992, p. A8. See, also, Anastaplo, *The Artist as Thinker*, pp. 322-30. See, for a useful survey of discussions of "restrictions on bigoted expression," Mark A. Graber, "Old Wine in New Bottles: The Constitutional Status of Unconstitutional Speech," *Vanderbilt Law Review*, 48: 349 (1995). "In Britain [a] prohibition on the cruder forms of racist speech forced racists to seek more sophisticated formulations of their propaganda . . . . The result, apparently, was an increase in the appeal of racist propaganda." *Ibid.*, 288 n.194 (quoting from David Kretzmer, "Freedom of Speech and Racism," *Cardozo Law Review*, 8: 445, 507 [1987]). A key question underlying discussions of this subject is as to who the true realists among us are. Sometimes, for example, it is realistic (that is, prudent) to be respectful of the healthier pieties of a decent people. See notes 29, 31, and 33, above. See, also, note 20, above.

concern of our "freedom of speech" protection. It is not difficult to imagine situations in which the offensive speech we permit so poisons the social atmosphere as to make it difficult for controversial speech to function as we need it to do. Thus, controversial speech may be subverted by that offensive speech which we may be reluctant to regulate (however much it may deserve it) lest that regulation lead to unfortunate curtailments of our much-needed controversial speech.

Is it unreasonable in our circumstances to insist upon (and if need be, to restore) a level of civility that makes it possible to have the most productive discussion of controversial issues, including the issue of how gross breaches of civility should be dealt with by the community? It should be remembered that the very men who recognized in the Constitution and the First Amendment the merits of unfettered debate of public issues recognized as well that decorum in political discourse should be insisted upon (and protected by firm sanctions) for the sake of productive debate. They did not allow themselves to be paralyzed by the assumption that since there may be politically-motivated differences of opinion about what decorum is, they should never insist upon it. It may not speak well of our way of life if there should now be so much incivility among us that we are moved to consider curbing it by means of laws and regulations — but it may be even worse not to try to do something about it at once (whether unofficially or officially) even as we search out its underlying causes. Better than the typical campus hate-speech code, for example, is the understanding that "this is not the way we do things here." Academic authorities should be confident enough to stand for commonsensical standards.

v.

No matter how justified, if not even obliged, we may be in discouraging certain ways of talking to and about each other, the subjects about which contemporary campus hate-speech codes are most concerned have to remain accessible to frank and vigorous public discussion if we are to know and to choose sensibly what we are doing. This public discussion has to address one serious argument against such codes, or certain applications of them: they do tend to insulate several important matters from sustained examination.

The typical campus hate-speech code today is concerned, it seems, primarily with what are described as racist, sexist, and homophobic insults. No doubt, many unfair, if not even destructive, things are said about the vulnerable people against whom such insults are directed, including racial and ethnic minorities, women, and homosexuals. But implicit in hate speech is sometimes a plausible challenge either with respect to contemporary pieties or with respect to those on whose behalf those pieties are invoked.

We can recall how difficult, if not even dangerous, it sometimes was at various times since the Second World War to challenge the accepted pieties in this country with respect to Communism, the Soviet Union, and the Cold War. The inhibitions encountered here did us all a disservice, leading to determined misallocations of vast resources and to the questionable sacrifice of many lives, undermining thereby our sense of national purpose. We would have been far better off if our political discussions had been less inhibited, however dubious some of the suppressed arguments of that time may have been.

Similarly, we may need to hear unpopular (and often wrongheaded, if not even wronghearted) criticisms of certain racial, sexual and other opinions and practices. There *are* opinions and practices here, some of them calling into question the very nature of nature, that are highly questionable themselves.

If we cannot deal adequately with the style or manner of offensive speech, which does seem to me a legitimate concern of the community, without also running a serious risk of ruling out discussion of certain controversial issues, then that may be a good reason for staying away from the regulation of style and manner, however much we may be entitled to deal with them. Prudential judgment is called for here, not constitutional adjudication. One practical safeguard is evenhandedness in making and applying the campus regulations relied upon to curb offensiveness. This means that both the good guys and the bad have to be reminded of the requirements of civility.

vi.

No matter what we do, however, it seems likely that we will probably have to put up with some offensive speech that is oblivious to (if not even provoked by) social pressure. Certainly, the typical hate-speech code is easily circumvented by the wary culprit. Further complicating these matters is the likelihood that those resisting suppression of gross incivility will be able to present themselves as champions of our traditional freedom of speech, which is hardly what is relevant here. The unregulated, perhaps unregulatable, incivility we can expect will probably have to be countered by both counseling and contempt. Also, we should try to put ourselves in a condition to make as good a use as possible of such incivility, particularly by analyzing and discussing what accounts for the disturbing and yet instructive hatred that is on exhibit.

What *does* account for such hatred? Often, the primary cause is the state of the soul of the hater, including the inadequacies of his education and social training. But we should not always assume that the conventional targets of hatred are themselves without deficiencies, or seeming deficiencies. Such deficiencies should be taken seriously, if only for the good of those who are targeted, who may be the way they are (susceptible to self-destructive outbursts of their own latent hostility from time to time) largely because of the crippling effects of decades if not even centuries of mistreatment. Need I add the obvious, that the better and more self-knowing the targets become, the less effect is hate speech likely to have either on them or on others?

vii.

We should take care, in opposing either hate speech or hate-speech codes, not to deny that there are such things as gross incivility and widespread corruption, that there are enduring standards of the good and the bad and of the beautiful and the ugly to be drawn upon here, and that the community, whether formally or informally, is entitled and sometimes even obliged to apply those standards for the sake of a responsible freedom. If we deny these standards and judgments, we deny also the possibility of a serious community — and we in effect dismiss freedom itself as purposeless.

Hatred is critical in these matters. Sometimes that hatred is really self-hate or suicidal. We should also recognize that it is not good for either the hater or his victim that the hater conduct himself as he does. This means that we should be careful not to resort to hatred ourselves in acting as vigorously as need be either against hate speech or against those who would curb hate speech by self-defeating measures.

PART TWO

REMINDERS OF
THE DREADFUL CONSEQUENCES
THAT HATEFUL SPEECH CAN HAVE

I.

THE FATE OF THE JEWS IN GREECE AND ITALY DURING THE SECOND WORLD WAR[40]

Do listen to what happened to me, so that you may see that I would not yield even to one man against the just course of action because of a fear of death, even if I were to perish by refusing to yield . . . . I, men of Athens, never held any office in the city except for being once on the Council. And it happened that our tribe, Antiochis, held the prytany when you wished to judge the ten generals (the ones who did not pick up the men from the naval battle) as a group — unlawfully, as it seemed to all of you in the time afterwards. I alone of the prytanes opposed your doing anything against the laws then, and I voted against it. And although the orators were ready to indict me and arrest me, and you were ordering and shouting, I supposed that I should run the risk with the law and the just rather than side with you because of fear of prison or death when you were counselling unjust things.

Now this was when the city was still under the democracy. But again, when oligarchy came to be, the Thirty [Tyrants] summoned five of us into the Tholos, and they ordered us to arrest Leon the Salaminian and bring him from Salamis to die. They ordered many others to do many things of this sort, wishing that as many as possible would be implicated in the responsibility. Then, however, I showed again, not in speech but in deed, that I do not even care about death in any way at all — if it is not too crude to say so — but that my whole care is to commit no unjust or impious deed. That government, as strong as it was, did not shock me into doing anything unjust. When we came out of the Tholos, the other four went to Salamis and arrested Leon, but I departed and went home. And perhaps I would have died because of this, if that government had not been quickly overthrown.

— Socrates[41]

---

[40]   This talk was prepared for delivery at a Conference on the Holocaust in Southern Europe. This Conference, sponsored by the National Italian-American Foundation, was held in Chicago, Illinois, October 7, 1994. This talk has been published, with the editorial assistance of Themi Vasils and Theodora Vasils, in *The Greek Star*, Chicago, Illinois, January/February 1995.

[41]   Plato, *Apology of Socrates* 32A-E (in the translation by Thomas G. West and Grace Starry West published by the Cornell University Press).

i.

The fate of the Jews in Southern Europe during the Second World War differed from country to country — and, indeed, as in Greece, their fate could differ from one region to another in the same country.   One constant factor everywhere in Occupied Europe was the insane determination of the Nazi savages to slaughter all the Jews that they could get their hands on.   How much murdering the Nazis could do depended, primarily, on the circumstances of the Jews in a place and on the degree of cooperation that the Nazis were able to get from the local population in their merciless campaigns against Jews.[42]

The Greeks, by and large, did not collaborate with the Germans during the Second World War — and for this they suffered grievously.   The German army was never welcome in Greece.   Nor, of course, had the Italian army which invaded Greece in October 1940 been welcome — but the Italians (whose hearts were not in that invasion) could be repelled by the Greeks, at least until the Germans came to the rescue of their humiliated ally.   Greece could not do much (even with some help from the British) to withstand the massive Germany attack — but it, after having been obliged to surrender to the Germans in April 1941, could maintain significant Resistance efforts throughout the long and brutal German and Bulgarian Occupation that followed.[43]

The most vulnerable Jews in Greece were always those in Salonika, "the Jerusalem of the Balkans" and the most eminent Sephardic settlement in Europe, where Jews had lived in large numbers since their expulsion from Spain in 1492.

---

[42]   See, on both the antecedents and the atrocities of the Nazis in Europe, Arno J. Meyer, *Why Did the Heavens Not Darken?   The "Final Solution" in History* (New York: Pantheon Books, 1988).

[43]   See, on the Greek Spirit, my contribution to the article on Modern Greece in the current edition of the *Encyclopedia Britannica*.

(It has been estimated that when Greece was overrun in 1941, between 5,000 and 6,000 Jews lived in the Bulgarian zone of occupation; about 13,000 lived in the Italian zone; and more than 55,000 lived in the German zone, which included Salonika and its closely-knit and highly conspicuous community of 53,000 Jews, or more than two-thirds of the Jews in Greece.[44]) It proved to be a fairly simple matter for the Germans, in early 1943, to begin to trap the Jews in Salonika for shipment to their death camps in Eastern Europe, particularly Auschwitz. The Germans did not need, for this deadly operation, the cooperation of the Greeks, however much the worst elements among the Greeks (as elsewhere) were available for the most horrible deeds. What the Germans did need in Salonika, as was often the case elsewhere, was the ignorance among Jews as to what fate was intended for them, an ignorance made possible in large part by the very enormity of the evil that had been planned by the Nazis.[45]

The safest places in Greece for Jews, or for other Greeks hunted by the Germans, were probably in those areas of the country that were controlled by the Greek Resistance. The next safest places for Jews and others were in the parts of Greece occupied by the Italian army. (This was true also in the parts of France and Croatia occupied by the Italians.[46]) The Greeks, however much they resented the unjustified Italian invasion of their country in 1940, recognized that the Italian zone of occupation was administered far more compassionately than either the Bulgarian zone or the German zone, so much so that the Germans came

---

[44]   See Raul Hilberg, *The Destruction of the European Jews* (Chicago: Quadrangle Books, 1961), p. 442.

[45]   I suggest the comprehensive madness and hence the "unbelievability" of that evil in my discussion of the 1945-1946 Nuremberg Trial. See Anastaplo, "On Trial," pp. 977-94.

[46]   See, for example, Leon Poliakov and Jacques Sabille, *Jews Under the Italian Occupation* (New York: Howard Fertig, 1983), p. 160. See also, note 91, below.

to have "serious doubts of the 'sincerity of implementation' [of German anti-Jewish measures] on the part of the Italians."[47]   (Yet even here there were anomalies. For example, the Bulgarian government which cooperated so readily with the Germans in hunting down Jews in Greece was reluctant to deliver the Jews in Bulgaria to the Nazis.   Similarly, in Vichy France, the French collaborationist government was, at least for awhile, far more protective of French Jews than it was of foreign Jews living in France.)

Outside of Salonika the Jews of Greece were much more difficult to identify — and the Christian Greeks were not eager to be of help to the Germans there. Not that most Greeks were specially concerned about the fate of their Jews. What was done on behalf of those Jews seems to have been a part of what was done by Greeks generally to resist and frustrate the foreign tyrants who had imposed their will upon their country. I have been told that the level of anti-Semitism (that is, hatred of Jews) has always been low in Greece. (While I was growing up in St. Louis and in Southern Illinois in the 1930s, I could hear Turks occasionally disparaged by my immigrant parents, but never the Jews.) Jewish officers were known to have distinguished themselves in the gallant defense of Greece in 1940-1941 and thereafter in the Resistance; this made it difficult for the Germans and their collaborators to portray the Jews in Greece in the way they were portrayed elsewhere — as bourgeois, exploitive, cosmopolitan and hence unpatriotic. Thus, in Greece, the Jews outside of Salonika had far more to fear from desperate Jewish leaders who were driven to cooperate with the Germans (as happened all too often in other countries as well) than they had to fear either from the Greeks or from many of the Italian occupiers in Greece. Perhaps it was inevitable, considering how much the sense of community has always meant to

---

[47]   Hilberg, *The Destruction of the European Jews*, p. 448.

Jews, that too many of their unreliable leaders would be trusted by Jews in the countries occupied by the Germans.[48]

ii.

It should not be surprising that the spirited Greeks would not cooperate with their German occupiers in any enterprise that the Germans set their hearts upon. What *is* remarkable is the effective opposition by the fairly easygoing Italians to various German initiatives (not least against the Jews) in Greece, France, Croatia, and Italy. Again and again, Italian diplomats, military officers, and even some Fascist bureaucrats (as well as the common soldier and the population at large) refused to help the Germans do the terrible things that they tried to do. One consequence of this was that eighty percent of the fifty thousand Italian Jews survived the war. The survival rate of the Italian Jews would probably have been lower, however, if the German occupation of Italy had lasted as long as did the German occupation of Greece, where (largely because of the deadly Salonika trap) no more than twenty percent of the Greek Jews survived. (It seems that perhaps half of the more than twenty thousand Jews in Greece outside of Salonika survived the War.)

It certainly helped the cause of humanity in Italy that there was in that country no concentration of distinctive-looking and foreign-sounding Jews such as there was in Salonika and Janina. (Also distinctive-looking, and hence vulnerable all over Europe, were the Gypsies, the forgotten victims of the Nazis.) To outsiders such as the Germans, the Jews of Italy were not obviously distinguishable from other Italians. By the time the Germans occupied Italy (after the post-Mussolini government surrendered to the Allies in the Fall of 1943),

---

[48]   See, for example, Rachel Dalven, "The Holocaust in Janina," *Journal of Modern Greek Studies*, vol. 2, no. 1 (1984), p. 87. See, on the Nazi manipulation of Jewish "leadership," Isaiah Trunk, *Judenrat: The Jewish Councils in Eastern Europe under Nazi Occupation* (New York: Macmillan, 1972).

most Italians were so opposed to the War that the Germans could not expect any reliable help from them. In fact, after September 1943, the Germans treated the Italians as another conquered people, even going so far as to gun down Italian troops who resisted them. About 640,000 Italian officers and men spent part of the War in German prison camps, where 30,000 of them died.[49] However blameworthy Italy may be for having helped make the Second World War possible, that country never threw itself anywhere into the racial programs of the Nazis. For one thing, a virulent anti-Semitism has never had deep roots in Italy where there has been a substantial Jewish presence since Roman times (that is, even before Christianity came to Italy). However questionable official Vatican policies with respect to the Jews may have at times been during the War, many Italians (including priests, monks, and nuns) provided refuges and other help for Jews sought by the Nazis, often at the risk of their own lives. All this is not to deny, of course, that there were some Italians, just as there were some Greeks, who did things in collaboration with the Nazis that should not have been done by anyone.

What does seem to have deep roots among Italians is a sense of humanity — and the beneficiaries of this, during the Second World War, included (as I have said) the Jews, the Greeks, the French, and the Croatians. In fact, it can be added, the mainland Italians may be by and large the gentlest people in Europe today. (This is reflected in how they treat their children. This is also reflected in the fact that most Italian Jews decided after the War "to remain in Italy rather than emigrate to Israel or the United States, as most German and Eastern

---

[49]   See Susan Zucotti, *The Italians and the Holocaust* (New York: Basic Books, 1987), p. 7.

European Jews did."[50]) Certainly, the Italians are the gentlest of the peoples that ring the Mediterranean. How they got to be this way can be debated. (Machiavelli, long ago, singled out the influence of the Roman Catholic Church in these matters.) Still, another question is whether such gentleness is always in the service of the common good: a determined toughness may sometimes be called for. (Here, too, Machiavelli can be instructive. This is related to Mussolini's determination to harden the Italian character by exposure to wars.) Too much, or the wrong kind, of gentleness can lead to intolerable conditions which open the way to a Strong Man who promises deliverance but who delivers oppression. On the other hand, if the Greeks had more of the Italian gentleness, they probably would not have subjected themselves to the cruel civil war that followed the Second World War in Greece.

Thus, the Jews of Italy, like those of Denmark, owed their survival in such large numbers to special circumstances, not the least of which was the character of the peoples among whom they happened to be living when the Nazis made their evil demands. One suspects that Italian gentleness would not have sufficed in Denmark, where a highly disciplined evacuation program had to be organized. One also suspects that Danish integrity would not have worked as well in Italy, where geographical and social circumstances made an almost instinctive "bending of the law" and passive resistance more effective.[51]

---

[50]   Alexander Stille, *Benevolence and Betrayal: Five Italian Jewish Families under Fascism* (New York: Summit Books, 1991), p. 13.

[51]   See, on civil disobedience, Anastaplo, *The American Moralist*, p. 537. See, for extended accounts of the slaughter of the Jews during the Second World War, Gerald Reitlinger, *The Final Solution: The Attempt to Exterminate the Jews of Europe 1939-1945* (New York: Thomas Yoseloff, 1968); Lucy S. Dawidowicz, *The War Against the Jews 1933-1945* (New York: Holt, Rinehart and Winston, 1975).

iii.

I have been asked to suggest on this occasion what we can do to protect ourselves in the future from such systematic atrocities as the Nazis inflicted upon the world a half century ago. I suspect that the term *protect* can lead us astray here. *Protection* tends to emphasize anticipating the sorts of things that the Nazis did and then setting up barriers against them. We are tempted to adopt this defensive approach when we recall that critical to the devastation that the Nazis wrought was the fact that few (if any) Europeans expected the Germans to do, so systematically and on so large a scale, the barbaric things which they certainly did. So despicable were the horrible things ordered by the Nazis that they usually did not dare admit even to their own people what they were doing. (It is destined to remain a mystery how many knew what and when. What is not a mystery is why few ever wanted to be publicly recognized as personally responsible for the Nazi atrocities. There is something reassuringly natural about this.)

No doubt, something is to be said for a useful wariness, including an awareness of the monstrous things that human beings can indeed do to one another. But wariness should not be permitted to deteriorate into either paranoia or passivity, both of which can be corrosive by constantly exposing one's imagination to horrors. One should be cautious, that is, about either expecting or dwelling upon the worst, generation after generation. This can be routinely crippling, whereas the monstrous rarely appears. In these matters, that is, constant apprehensiveness, a spirit of surrender, and a sense of perpetual grievance all tend to become obstacles to a proper maturation.

A far healthier approach here, and usually more truly practical, is to encourage and equip the finest human beings among us. A morbid preoccupation either with erecting barriers against the worst possible eventuality or with feeling helpless in expectation of dreadful things can keep the best souls from flourishing.

The role of chance in such matters is evident, even distressingly evident, to anyone familiar with Holocaust stories. *Being good*, which includes having the capacity to figure out and then to do whatever is called for, is probably the most reliable protection in a variety of circumstances. One needs to be able to identify accurately and to think sensibly about the unpredictable challenges one happens to confront if one is to improvise effectively in the extreme cases that do chance to arise. Such effectiveness depends upon being guided in the face of the monstrous by a sense of decency and upon being strengthened in the most dangerous situations by a sense of honor. It should be emphasized that the proper response to evil programs varies from place to place and from time to time. Automatic responses in these matters are likely to be self-defeating. It also helps, if one is to conduct oneself as one should in response to the most terrible demands, to keep within reasonable limits that oppressive "fear of prison or death" which Socrates warned against. The role here of a sound education cannot be overestimated, however discouraging the 1933-1945 experiences of the highly cultured German people may have been.

In any event, it is prudent to notice that the worst atrocities organized in the 1940s by the Nazis were done under cover of war. Therefore it is also prudent, especially at a time when military technology and modern governments can be so devastating, for us to be most reluctant to countenance recourse to war by anyone, however much power it may be our duty to hold in reserve in order to discourage the unruly. Men and women of good will should be heartened somewhat, as well as instructed, upon contemplating and even cherishing the salutary (however flawed) gentleness of the remarkably good-natured Italian people. Also to be contemplated, with both awe and gratitude, are the great

Jewish people who have contributed so much to civilizing the Western World, something that resentful savages can never understand.[52]

---

[52]   See, for example, *Deuteronomy* 4: 1, 5-8; 1 *Samuel* 17: 1-51; *Proverbs* 29: 18. See, on the case for supporting Israel, Anastaplo, *Human Being and Citizen*, pp. 155-59. See, on the power of gentleness, a 1965 poem by Sara Prince Anastaplo inspired by the bells of donkeys and goats:

Delphi

Delphi is the sound of bells —
Beaten copper, twisted thin,
Folded, nailed with metal shells
Struck by hide and skeleton,
In rhythms moved by legs.

The mountain's thrust, the birds' wild wings
Scarce touch the air that bears their stress.
This world declares that gentleness
Is strength and, bell-like, sings.

II.

WHERE DOES ONE START? ON THE UNITED STATES, THE BALKANS, AND ISLAM[53]

> . . . To be revenged was more in demand [among the Corcyreans] than never to have received injury. . . . The cause of all this [deadly division within cities] is desire of rule, out of avarice and ambition; and the zeal of contention from these two proceeding. For such as were of authority in the cities, both of the one and the other faction, preferring under decent titles, one *the political equality of the multitude*, the other *the moderate aristocracy*; though in words they seemed to be servants of the public, they made it in effect but the prize of their contention: and striving by whatsoever means to overcome, both ventured on most horrible outrages and prosecuted their revenges still farther without any regard of justice or the public good, but limiting them, each faction, by their own appetite and stood ready, whether by unjust sentence, or with their own hands, when they should get power, to satisfy their present spite.
>
> — Thucydides[54]

i.

Our assignment this morning is to consider the feasibility of foreign intervention in Bosnia and Herzegovina. One form of our intervention in the desperate Bosnian situation of which we all, or almost all, must approve is that of informed discussion of the issues with a view to determining what, if anything,

---

[53]   This talk was prepared for delivery at the beginning of "A Day for Bosnia" Conference at the University of Chicago, Chicago, Illinois, February 8, 1993. Preparation of this talk was aided considerably by telephone conversations with Leo Paul S. de Alvarez, Laurence Berns, Maurice F. X. Donohue, Harry V. Jaffa, William H. McNeill, Charles Moskos, and John A. Murley. None of these scholars is responsible for what is said here.

[54]   Thucydides, *Peloponnesian War*, III, 82 (Thomas Hobbes translation).

can be done by outsiders.   Perhaps what we have to say here may be of immediate use for the beleaguered Bosnians, but about this we should not be too hopeful, considering how complicated the Balkan situation has long been and how limited the personal influence of most of us is likely to be.

Such discussions as we are embarking upon on this occasion are likely to be, for most of us, "academic" — but in the good sense of that term.   That is, we may become better equipped thereby to anticipate and deal with explosive situations in the future, well before they become as desperate as what we now see in Bosnia and her neighbors.   The future includes the possibility, if not the probability, of a confrontation between Christendom (including, for this purpose, Israel) and Islam — a worldwide confrontation which can make the Cold War pale by comparison.   In order to understand what goes on in such situations, where *does* one start?   Where does one start — both in one's actions of the moment and (with a view to actions, immediate and later) in one's attempt to understand what is going on?[55]

ii.

In these matters, one cannot truly understand if one cannot pass judgment. The moral dimension is usually an essential part of the more significant political crises we are likely to confront.   No discussion, in such circumstances, can be complete if one refuses to pass moral judgment once one has access to the relevant information that may be available.

Consider, for example, what Leslie H. Gelb, in last Thursday's *New York Times*, reports from Vitez, Bosnia and Herzegovina:[56]

---

[55]   See, for example, Anastaplo, *The Artist as Thinker*, p. 7.

[56]   Leslie H. Gelb, "Foreign Affairs," *New York Times*, February 4, 1993, p. A15.

. . . World attention is riveted on Sarajevo. Resisting the brutal Serbian siege, that ancient city has become the symbol of Muslim survival. But if Sarajevo is the heart and soul of old Bosnia, the interior is its whole body.

What I saw here over three days is hard for me to comprehend. You drive past a village of prosperous green farms, peaceful and quiet and peopled by Muslims, Croats and Serbs. You pass towns like Novi Travnik and see a mosque, a Catholic church, and a Greek Orthodox church within yards of one another. You also see burned-out houses smoking next to tidy, untouched farms. The killing and terror here is highly personalized, unlike the indiscriminate destruction of Sarajevo. . . .

Everything is hopelessly mixed and mixed up. The people all look like one Balkan family, at least to an outsider. They're all Slavs — tens of thousands intermarried and intermingled. They're all alike, except to each other. And for the differences they see, they kill each other.

Neighbors kill and rape neighbors here, as the world now knows. But more and more, "outsiders" come to these central villages to commit the crimes that familiar neighbors will not. . . . As the fighting spreads, the nasties of all ethnic stripes are taking control of everyday life. The guys with the guns become the police, who become the criminals and the terrorists.

Even the Vance-Owen peace talks breed more killing. All sides have stepped up the fighting to control more land — in the unlikely event of a peace settlement in Geneva.

Almost without exception, U.N. officials and soldiers here to help the Bosnians believe all sides are equally guilty. The U.N. soldiers I talked with believed deeply in their limited humanitarian mission — and argued vehemently that it would be insanity for the West to try to solve the problems here with force. . . .

Instructive as Mr. Gelb's report is, one reservation about it must be expressed if a reliable understanding of the situation is to be secured. It is not discriminating enough to suggest that "all sides are equally guilty." Thus, we should be able to assess and compare the virtues and vices — the defensible and the questionable conduct — of various of the parties acting in Bosnia and Croatia these days. Particularly to be regretted — and now I speak as one reared more than half a century ago in the Eastern Orthodox faith — particularly to be regretted is the fact that the worst offenders *this time around* seem to have been some of the leaders of the Serbs (who present themselves as more or less Eastern Orthodox in sympathy). This is not to suggest that the other parties to this ugly civil war within the former Yugoslavia have been without fault. I have emphasized *this time around*, since the Serbs are, in large part, responding viscerally to what has been done to them over the years, just as now we and many others will respond viscerally for some time to come to what the Serbs have been doing recently.

I myself found the Yugoslavs that I encountered, in a dozen trips by automobile or by train across the length of that beautiful country in the 1960s (usually on the way to or from Greece), to be lively, good natured, artistically adventurous, somewhat undisciplined, and apparently comfortable with one another despite their diversity. I also found them careful in what they said publicly about politics: perhaps this helped keep them from knowing, and ministering to, themselves in a salutary manner. Perhaps, that is, they should have been more candid in examining the deep-seated passions that are now out of control, thereby taking advantage of the domestic tranquility imposed for decades by the Tito regime. Would this have been possible? Certainly, the decent people of that region must now wish they had been able to give candor and good will an opportunity to bring out the best in the diverse peoples of Yugoslavia.

iii.

Can anything sensible be done now by us in the Balkans, considering how bloody-minded all too many among the contending parties have evidently become? This is the kind of question we face also when we consider the epidemics of killing to which we have become accustomed in our larger cities in this country. Immediately before the international community is the Vance-Owen cease-fire plan which proposes to pacify Bosnia by transforming her into a loose federation of ten nearly autonomous cantons. It is apparent to everyone that this is a seriously flawed plan, one that is not likely to work either very well or very long.

It testifies to how bad things are in that part of the world that this, or something like this, should be the best that intelligent and experienced men and women of good will, on the spot, are likely to come up with. Perhaps such an arrangement provides everyone a face-saving way of stopping the killing. Perhaps, that is, people in Bosnia are already sick enough of bloodshed and misery (of "horrible outrages") that any halfway plausible plan can be fastened upon, at least for awhile. (The factions that would dominate the various cantons can still be expected, in Bosnia as elsewhere, to continue both to violate one agreement after another and to maneuver for new positions — and all this in anticipation of more fighting later.)

Even an uncertain ceasefire could allow passions to cool somewhat, which might lead in turn to a better plan being developed by the more sober and sensible members of the dozen or so Balkan communities with a stake in a long-term settlement among themselves, if *they* should get a chance to do something. Whether the development of financial and commercial relations, especially as the European economic union increases its influence, can eventually tame religious and other passions must remain to be seen. It also remains to be seen whether the explosive Wilsonian "principle" of self-determination can be tamed as well.

It is hard to see that American or United Nations firepower, as distinguished from peacekeeping personnel, can be put to effective use at this time whatever the possibilities may have been last summer. Many experts do have the impression that the United States, Western Europeans, and *Russians* should have moved earlier and decisively to smother the first signs of conflict in Yugoslavia. One must wonder what the incredibly expensive NATO forces that have been built up for decades are good for now if they are not to be used at the outset of a crisis such as this. It is a piece of bad luck that all this has been happening at a time that finds the President of France obliged to be as limited as he now is politically: a more vigorous man in his position might have been able to move in a sustained manner to head off *these* troubles in the Balkans, at least for the time being. Others can regret that Margaret Thatcher has not been available to act here — but neither the Falklands War nor the Gulf War, whatever one thinks of those exercises, provides a model for what has long been needed in the Balkans. Even so, Mr. Gelb concluded his column from Sarajevo in yesterday's *New York Times* with this plea:[57]

> The U.S. is revered and feared here, and Europe awaits a strong and wise lead from Washington. But this dead city with its live people somehow hanging on — a mere hour and a half from London or Paris by plane — is ultimately the ward of all civilized nations.
>
> This week, Western powers must push on Serbia with full diplomatic weight for an immediate cease-fire around Sarajevo. Time is of the essence, and only threat of force, not more toothless envoys, can save Sarajevans.

Sarajevo, it should never be forgotten, is where the Thirty Years War of 1914-1945 began — and not accidentally.

iv.

The obvious inadequacies of the Vance-Owen plan, however salutary the work of these "toothless envoys" may turn out to be, do testify to the unfortunate history of the Balkans. I have singled out, as most observers have, the recent misconduct of some of the Serbs. Dreadful as that conduct is, that of some of the Croats, who shamelessly collaborated with the Nazi occupiers of Yugoslavia during the Second World War, was far worse. Jews and Gypsies, as well as Serbs, were enthusiastically victimized by the worst elements among the Croats during the Occupation, obscuring thereby the contributions that Croats made also

---

[57]   Leslie H. Gelb, "Foreign Affairs," *New York Times*, February 7, 1993, p. E21.

to the heroic resistance that Yugoslavia put up against her German and Austrian invaders.

The Bosnian Muslims today (some of whose parents and grandparents, it is to be regretted, helped the Roman Catholic Croats and the Nazis in their bestiality, just as earlier they had collaborated with the Austrians in *their* occupation) have centuries of Christian grievances against them to contend with, going back to the troubling conversions to Islam when the Turks conquered much of the Balkans half a millennium ago. Here at least, it sometimes seems, Serbs and Croats have a common cause as Christian patriots. We can see displayed by them toward Muslims some of the passions displayed (elsewhere in the Balkans) by the Greeks toward the Turks down to our time, passions that we can be reminded of in this country whenever Greek-American leaders speak about the current lamentable situation in Cyprus.

But "Cyprus" should also remind us that such situations are often far more complicated than partisans are able to recognize. Thus, Greek-Americans tend to forget that the disturbing occupation of much of Cyprus by Turkey was precipitated in 1974 by an invasion of Cyprus launched by the Greek government. That military government in Athens was able to stay in power as long as it did, and to do the enduring mischief it did in the Eastern Mediterranean, in large part because of that government's powerful support in Washington by most of the influential Greek-Americans of that day. Much of this has been forgotten by the Greek-American community of our day.[58] I suspect that each of the factions in Bosnia, Serbia, and Croatia has similarly forgotten, if it ever recognized, its own questionable contributions to the disasters that have been repeatedly visited upon that beautiful land. Even if a general Balkan war would not again threaten the

---

[58]   See, on the disastrous military government in Athens, Anastaplo, *Human Being and Citizen*, pp. 3-6; *The American Moralist*, pp. 501-15.

general stability of all of Europe, "realistic" outsiders must resist the temptation (here, just as elsewhere around the world) to let the mutual slaughter continue until the various factions finally come to their senses. Humanitarian, as well as geopolitical, concerns counsel the genuine realist to do what can be done now to give "peace" a chance.

v.

It is often the case that the victims in one place or time show up as victimizers elsewhere. In more ways than one, it can be hard to know where one should start — and where and how one should stop.

In Bosnia, the victims most cruelly imposed upon these days seem to be the Muslims, partly because they are caught up in ancient feuds between Croats and Serbs. In other countries, of course, Muslims (albeit different Muslims) are the aggressors. This may be seen in what has been happening for several years now to animists and Christians in the Sudan and to Armenians in the former Soviet Union. It may also be seen in what happened to the Armenians in Turkey early in this century. This, along with the checkered history of the Turks in the Balkans, makes somewhat troublesome any offers of aid from Turkey for the Bosnian Muslims. Also troublesome is any suggestion that the Iranians and the Saudi Arabians, neither of whom are known for toleration, should champion the cause of the Bosnian Muslims. The Salmon Rushdie scandal is instructive here. The ways that Muslims can go wrong, on their own, are suggested by what they have been doing among themselves in Somalia during the last decade and what they did among themselves during the Iran-Iraq war, a war that rivalled in its mindless destructiveness what Christians were able to do among themselves during the First World War and what the Greeks were able to do among themselves during their Civil War in the 1940s.[59]

I have already referred to the perils of a worldwide confrontation between Christendom and Islam, a confrontation that would dramatize and perhaps intensify the fundamental differences about the meaning and status of revelation, liberty, property, justice, community, equality, and philosophy that there were behind the East-West standoff during the Cold War. Where the Russians and Chinese would eventually come down in such a new confrontation remains to be seen. In the short run, we should be concerned lest hardliners among the Russians, exploiting Moscow's historic affinity with the Serbs, be able to revive aspects of the Cold War with the West. No people in Europe can benefit for long if Russia's current pro-West policy should be repudiated.[60]

Whatever the grand sweep of worldwide clashes may be, however, the suffering Bosnian Muslims are entitled to be judged on their own merits, an entitlement that follows from one of the cherished principles of the West. These distinctively European Muslims (who are almost as Slavic as the Serbs and the Croats) have long been part of a cosmopolitan, relaxed Islamic community, centered upon Sarajevo, a charming, pleasure-savoring but proud city. The saddest thing perhaps about the Bosnian debacle is that that region had been one of those rare places where vital religious and ethnic differences could be routinely submerged in the cause of humanity. Bosnia exhibited what Yugoslavia was meant to be: an attractive union of Slavs liberated from foreign masters. Particularly instructive to this end is what the greatest Greek storyteller of this century, Nikos Kazantzakis, had to say (as in his *Freedom or Death* novel) about the need for the Greeks to recognize the humanity of the Turks. Certainly, it

---

[59]   See, on Islamic thought, note 25, above.

[60]   See, for example, Anastaplo, *The American Moralist*, pp. 555-69; "On Freedom," pp. 630-44.

does not help to moderate potentially dangerous Muslim passions around the world to have so attractive an Islamic minority as that in Bosnia (however much it may have overreached itself) subjected to the savagery we have all been witnessing. This is not to deny, however, the questionableness of the decision to try to turn Bosnia into an independent country: if a multi-ethnic Yugoslavia was impractical, how could a much smaller multi-ethnic Bosnia hope to prosper?

In these matter it is prudent to be reminded of what Machiavelli says about any people who cannot "rest" because of the fierce memories and intense longings that they harbor. (See *The Prince*, Chapter 5.) The humane and perhaps most practical way of dealing with this condition is to try to teach people that such memories do not really matter as much as other things in the light of which their longings can properly be blended with the longings that others have. Aspirations grounded in self-evident truths and "certain unalienable Rights" should replace memories and longings shaped by "accident and force."[61] This is what the American regime stands for, not only here but to some extent around the world as well.

vi.

The principal alternative to what the United States does stand for, unless a benevolent despotism holds sway, is the periodic release of the worst passions that human beings are capable of. We can be reminded, as by Thucydides' account of the Corcyrean debacle during the Peloponnesian War, of what *can* happen when the wraps are taken off. (Thucydides, I notice in passing, is the greatest student ever of Balkan affairs.)

It should be evident in these matters that, after awhile, it does not help to keep score. There is always another atrocity that your opponents can be

---

[61]   See the Declaration of Independence and *Federalist* No. 1 (opening paragraph).

remembered to have committed, thereby justifying what your side is doing now and provoking what they will do next. The tortured history of the Balkans reminds us, if reminders we need, what sometimes has to happen if there is to be any kind of peace: things can get so bad that an amnesty has to be resorted to, a deliberate forgetting of grievances. This was done, for example, by the Athenians in order to stop the terrible bloodletting within their city that followed the Peloponnesian War.

Such deliberate forgetting does not depend upon a disavowal of differences between good and bad. Rather, it depends upon doing what has to be done to preserve enough of the good to permit civilization to reestablish itself. Especially to be guarded against somehow, as more and more wretched situations around the world happen to come to our attention, is what has been identified as "compassion burnout." Also to be guarded against is the aloofness that can be promoted by the recognition that it can be a matter of chance where and how we get interested and involved in other peoples' troubles. The fact that we cannot do "everything" should not leave us doing nothing, especially when challenged by Hitlerian programs of extermination.

vii.

We may well wonder (as scholars and statesmen will be wondering for decades) what the Cold War, or at least our failure to prepare properly for its end, contributed to the debacle in Bosnia and to even more dangerous disintegration elsewhere, including in parts of the former Soviet Union.

How did Josef Broz Tito manage to control, to the extent that he did, the divergent factions in Yugoslavia? Should not the more sensible people in the various communities there, knowing their history and reconciled to their geography, have built upon what Tito managed to do? Or did the often-brutal Tito only make matters worse, neglecting problems and building up pressures that would eventually lead to an explosion? Did he lose thereby a half-century of opportunity following upon the traumas of the Second World War? Can a better use be made, by men and women of good will, of the current traumas?[62]

Much is to be said in such circumstances for the larger political federations (such as Yugoslavia) that tend to make local passions obsolete or at least to cancel them out. (Consider, in the light of the teaching of *Federalist No. 10*, how an Israeli-Jordanian federation could bear on the chronic Palestinian problem.) Marxism did offer a universalism of sorts, however subverted it was in practice by personal ambition and self-seeking. Universalism, even when spurious, can keep at bay, at least for awhile, a tribalism which may be even more deadly, especially when fueled by religious passions.

Still, it is well to notice that what we should condemn as tribalism draws upon, however much it distorts, those familiar sentiments and intimate relations that make life rich, meaningful, and even joyful.

viii.

It is imprudent in these situations to fail to appreciate that matters can become even worse than they already are. We should take care, that is, not to insist upon too much as we try to stop that disturbing slide down to total disaster in which the Balkans find themselves at this time.

What such a slide can descend to (with Kosovo and Macedonia next in line?) may be seen in what the Nazis did throughout Europe, not least in

---

[62]   See, on the dreams and passions to be reckoned with in that part of the world, Rebecca West's remarkable 1941 report, *Black Lamb and Grey Falcon: A Journey Through Yugoslavia*. See, on the dependence of the fighting in Bosnia upon the arms and ideology of Greater Serbia, Michael Ignatieff, "Homage to Bosnia," *New York Review of Books*, April 21, 1994, p. 3. See, on the case that can be made for the Serbs today, Charles G. Boyd, "America Prolongs the War in Bosnia," *New York Times*, August 9, 1995, p. A15 (adapted from an article in the September-October 1995 issue of *Foreign Affairs*). Compare Eric Schmitt, "Spy Photos Indicate Mass Grave at Serb-Held Town, U.S. Says," *New York Times*, August 10, 1995, p. A1.

Yugoslavia, for which everyone there continues to pay more than a half-century later. It is a sad footnote to this history that the Germans of the 1990s, however well-intentioned this time around, contributed to the present precarious situation in the Balkans by their premature recognition of Slovenia and Croatia. Nor has the Vatican been as helpful as it should have been.

Rivaling the Nazis in monstrousness is what the Cambodian Marxists, known as the Khmer Rouge, did to their country in the 1970s, a disaster to which the shortsighted American policy with respect to Vietnam contributed. We are thus reminded, again and again, that there are monsters everywhere who are available to be recruited for dubious causes. (We can see them in our own society, in the form of serial killers and, even sadder to say, in the form of sadistic officers even in the better police forces.)

It is well to keep these extremes in view whenever we warn against "rewarding aggression." It is likely that no matter what settlements there should finally be imposed in the former Yugoslavia — grounded either in conquest or in good sense or in mutual exhaustion — considerable aggression will have been rewarded, whether aggression perpetrated in the 1990s or fifty years ago or even centuries ago. It will probably take a generation or two, in any event, before that troubled land once again has leaders who have not been either brutalized or compromised by both Fascist and Communist regimes. It remains to be seen whether the dream that once was Yugoslavia can ever make sense again.

ix.

I opened these remarks by drawing upon the proposition that one form of intervention we can usefully resort to, in Bosnia and elsewhere, is an examination of underlying issues, with an appreciation of how complicated things can be. One lesson of armed interventions in Cuba, Lebanon, Libya, Panama and Iraq by the United States has been that hit-and-run attacks cannot solve chronic problems.

Helpful as our military force and economic power can sometimes be, even more constructive are the principles of the American regime, including (but not limited to) that robust freedom of speech we are exercising here today. Fundamentally important, in circumstances such as those in which the fragmented Balkans now find themselves, are the lessons that the United States can teach the world about the basis upon which people of divergent ethnic origins and religious allegiances may live together peacefully and productively without having to rely upon despotism to protect them. We are what Yugoslavia aspired to be, however inadequate the principles of *that* regime seem to have been. It should be salutary for citizens of Serbian and of Croatian descent in this fortunate country of ours, just as for citizens of Greek and of Turkish descent here, to testify to people in "the old country" that it *is* possible to get along with ancestral enemies on the basis of the truly universalizable principles of the American regime. It remains to be seen whether those principles will be subverted among us both by the relativism of liberals and by the fundamentalism of conservatives.

Still another set of principles, which the American political regime was not the first to implement, are those which teach human beings that among those most benefitted when just and decent actions are insisted upon are those unfortunate men and women who might otherwise disgrace themselves and endanger their descendants by indulging in shameful atrocities.

We return to our opening question by asking again, Where *does* one start? Usually, it should be answered, one should start with one's own soul and the souls of those whom one holds most dear. *Principiis obsta.*

III.

THE NEEDS OF A FREE PEOPLE: REFLECTIONS ON THE OKLAHOMA CITY BOMBING[63]

E Pluribus Unum

— Seal of the United States

i.

Critical to any serious inquiry about the First Amendment and its "freedom of speech [and] of the press" have been, as we have seen this semester, questions about what must be believed and done if we are to continue to benefit from our perhaps unprecedented liberty. The emphasis has been placed in our inquiry upon the political discourse that was traditionally considered primary to freedom of speech protection, rather than upon the "freedom of expression" which is made so much of today. Neither unlawful action nor the use of speech for the furtherance of unlawful acts was anticipated by the Framers of the First Amendment as the object of their concerns. Nor would they have had any sympathy with attempts to justify unlawful acts as forms of protected *expression*, however much they themselves may have resorted at times to unlawful acts in resisting tyrannical authority.

There is, we have seen, nothing automatic about the way that the system of freedom of speech works for our benefit. Rather, our system depends upon effective responses, by sensible and informed citizens, to the abuses of freedom

---

[63]   This talk was prepared for delivery at the final meeting of a First Amendment course at the Loyola University School of Law, Chicago, Illinois, April 25, 1995.

of speech that are probably inevitable. Such responses are more likely when the community is aware of its prerogatives as well as of its limitations and when citizens are aware of their duties as well as of their rights.

Dreadful acts, such as the bombing of a Federal Government office building in Oklahoma City last Wednesday [April 19], can put our principles to the test as we try to determine what a free people may do to control the abuses of liberty, a people that knows why it is obliged to run the risks that it does. Among the risks run are the terrible things that may be done by a minority — by often pathetic people — who really do not know what they are doing.

ii.

A few days before the Oklahoma City bombing, I happened to give a talk, at a legal scholarship panel in Philadelphia, about the outbursts of violence that we have been witnessing around the world. Particular emphasis was placed by me on that occasion upon cults and their consequences. My talk [of April 15] opened with these remarks:[64]

> The recent murderous, indeed even devilish, attack upon Tokyo subway-train passengers, evidently by an apocalyptic cult, reminds us that it is not all "fun and games" when bizarre opinions are taken to heart by single-minded people. Some fanatics in Japan are prepared, it seems, to kill off thousands of their unsuspecting fellow citizens by the use of nerve gas and other toxic agents.

> We are also reminded by such eruptions of the risks run because of the toleration that has become fashionable around the globe, beginning perhaps with the attractive religious toleration developed since the Enlightenment in Western Europe and the United States. The public's ability and duty to supervise are disparaged these days, including any tendency there may be to be "judgmental."

---

[64]   The April 15, 1995 Philadelphia talk drawn upon here is to be published in Anastaplo, "Lessons for the Student of Law: The Oklahoma Lectures," *Oklahoma City University Law Review* (1995). The Philadelphia talk (at the American Culture Association annual convention) is entitled "Scientific Integrity, UFOs, and the Spirit of the Law." See, for a salutary reminder of how various vilified "cults" (such as Jesuits and Mormons) have eventually become respectable among us, John T. Biermans, *The Odyssey of New Religious Movements: Persecution, Struggle, Legitimation* (Lewiston, New York: Edwin Mellen Press, 1986).

. . . Many more aberrations can be expected in the decade ahead, especially as the Millennium draws to an end: there is a great temptation, if not even compulsion, for some to make much of the fact that they happen to live at so special a moment in the vast stretches of human history.

Most of us, upon learning of one more or less peaceful aberration after another, are probably reassured by the observation, "Of course, no one takes such things seriously . . ." But we are brought up short now and then by still another outburst: a massacre, or a wave of suicides, or even genocide.

It does not suffice to counter the threats of the demented, fanatical and murderous only by physical and mechanical means (such as routine surveillance, police raids, and official punishments). Needed also, perhaps even more, are the restoring and reshaping of a sound public opinion. What is essential here is what the disaffected believe about their grievances and what the community at large believes about its prerogatives. Underlying a sound public opinion in these matters is the status of truth-seeking and of the truth itself, not least with respect to issues of justice and the common good.

The conclusion of my April 15th talk in Philadelphia included these remarks:

I return, however briefly, to the deadly cults with which I began. Have we not become accustomed to, if not comfortable with, manifestations (if only, usually, verbal manifestations) of the Satanic in our lives? . . . This toleration of the Satanic may be related to our inclination to put up with considerable licentiousness among us. (One may even be embarrassed these days if one has to speak publicly against licentiousness.)

We have become accustomed as well to having all kinds of bizarre notions promulgated among us without serious challenge — and some of these do have deadly consequences. Censorship, at least in our circumstances, is not a remedy — but neither is a "don't care" or a "none of our business" response.

The various atrocities we witness monthly, if not weekly, depend in large part upon beliefs about things that we should be able to say are simply not so. Thus, as examples, both the heaven-bound suicide-bomber and the man who devotes everything to his physical self-preservation are woefully mistaken about the nature of human life and of the world. Related to both of these delusions is our mania about guns.

Censorship has to be distinguished in practice from an insistence by the community upon sound opinions. The processes of the law, when pursued effectively, help discredit unsound opinions and help confirm common sense for the community at large. (We can see in the cancerous O. J. Simpson trial what happens when legal processes seem to be pursued without evident regard for their intended purpose.) Legal skepticism can be useful, but only if kept within proper limits.

Fundamental to a healthier state of affairs is a revived confidence by the community in its ability to distinguish between salutary and pernicious opinions and also in its right as well as its duty to encourage the salutary and to discourage the pernicious. Hard-headedness is needed here, but not mean-spiritedness. A salutary hard-headedness is promoted by the proper study of the law.

I noticed in my Philadelphia talk the limits of "physical and mechanical means" in dealing with the acts of "the demented, fanatical and murderous." Among these means is the resort to such ultimately self-defeating measures as the death penalty, something that will probably be politically impossible to forego in any Oklahoma City murder case following upon that dreadful bombing. It can be dramatic, and usefully so, to hunt down the perpetrators of atrocities, making it clear thereby that people who do evil things will surely be caught and punished. The eventual detection of the Oklahoma City bombers, on the basis of minute clues, could have somewhat the effect of divine justice. (This is reflected in the *Chicago Sun-Times* headline for April 22: "Feds Zero In.")

Even so, it can lead us astray to make too much of convicting and punishing the criminals in these matters. It is like relying too much upon physicians to take care of the health of the community, without addressing the opinions and hence the ways of life which routinely put people's health in jeopardy. There may even be something materialistic and hence shortsighted about placing the emphasis that we sometimes do upon trials and punishments. It can tacitly encourage people to do whatever can escape detection — that is, whatever people are fairly sure they "can get away with."

iii.

Often, of course, it can also help to address the causes of most crimes — the poverty, discrimination and other social conditions which contribute to so much of our ordinary crime today. But there are limits to any community's effectiveness in taking care of, by removing the occasions for, any grievances at home or abroad. There are times, it seems, that no community effort, even if undertaken in the utmost good faith, will satisfy everyone who threatens domestic tranquility, especially if some people continue to believe the things that they do. Thus, no matter how formidable the criminal justice system and no matter how compassionate the social welfare system, some tormented souls may still have to be dealt with, perhaps even by force.

The tormented need, among other things, instruction about how their grievances should be regarded and acted on by them. People do need to be held responsible for what they say, if only by the sensibleness and vigor of what is said by others in response to their complaints and threats. In this way, it can be hoped, the cause of civility is encouraged.

iv.

I indicated in my Philadelphia talk ten days ago that something more than addressing grievances and punishing criminality may be needed to discourage the most frightful actions about which we are concerned these days. This is especially so in a free society, where there are a high level of unimpeded mobility and virtually unlimited (and probably unlimitable) access to the ingredients with which lethal concoctions can be made, no matter what changes are likely to be tried in the methods available to law-enforcement agencies.

I was reminded of this yesterday morning as I went to a meeting in a public building just across from the NBC Tower. A van was parked alongside the building, with its tailgate open and in which could be seen a dozen bags, comparable to the bags in which the Oklahoma City fertilizer must have once been packed. Two men, evidently connected with the van, were standing alongside it and speaking earnestly in a foreign tongue. Such scenes must be repeated thousands if not hundreds of thousands of times in this country every day. Almost always, of course, the "suspicious" men involved are simply trying to make a living — and all of us would lead far poorer lives if every such situation that we notice had to be investigated further and evaluated.

What we need then — to develop an argument I made in Philadelphia — is to challenge (and thus to change, or at least to silence and neutralize) the opinions significantly responsible for frightful actions. The actions we are most concerned about are those that can be done by people with ordinary mental capacities, not by the more thoughtful or original people. The critical opinions of "ordinary people," about both "facts" and "values," have to be addressed.

But, it is sometimes said, the critical opinions here are those held by fundamentalists, whether of the Left or of the Right, whether secular or religious. And, it is also said, such fundamentalists cannot be reasoned with. Even so, are there not causes of, or foundations for, the opinions held by even the most zealous among us? After all, people are not born with such opinions. There are things upon which their opinions depend. Those things can often be dealt with, preferably respectfully, but always firmly.

The community, as community, has to take an interest in various beliefs. No beliefs should be immunized from public investigation simply because they happen to be regarded by some as fundamental. Of course, prudence has to be exercised in addressing cherished opinions, lest unnecessary controversy be aroused. But the political and social consequences of any set of opinions, however labeled, are fair game for the conscientious citizen to examine and, if need be, to challenge or at least to shun. Among the matters that may at times be necessary to examine is what is said and meant by some people when they talk about God, Heaven, and the Apocalypse.

v.

Public-spirited challenges to dogmas accepted by some, especially dogmas of a pernicious tendency, may have to draw upon long-standing opinions that the decent, well-established community depends upon. We are in the realm here not of constitutional, legal or law-enforcement issues; rather, we are in the realm of education for political and moral health (to which a soundly-oriented religion might contribute).

It very much matters what is thought and said, or at least what is said, in the community about right and wrong, about friendship and hospitality, about justice, about honor and compassion, and about the duties owed to others. Serious discussions about these and like matters should be common in our public discourse, not least in the entertainment that we share.

People need to have impressed upon them the fact that they should not speak in certain atrocious ways without risking serious personal repercussions for themselves. They have to be shown what they are really doing — and that it is not good or manly or right, that it is not truly human, for them to continue to do so, however lawabiding they may generally be. We should not be shy about identifying and repudiating the bizarre opinions that we encounter. A certain rationality and humanity may be thereby appealed to. Of course, the lunatic may be difficult, if not impossible, to reach thus. But the lunatic is rarely effective; he, because of obvious aberrations, will usually be subject to detection and restraint before he can do much mischief.

Many of our misconceptions about the place of rights and duties in our scheme of things are related to a confusion among us between the public and the private. Some private things, such as one's personal sexual conduct, are now disclosed when they should not be; some public things, such as the education of children, are now treated as if they were completely private matters.

vi.

Among the things needed for promulgating and maintaining sound opinions about matters both public and private is a recognition of the role of nature in shaping, and in helping us to recognize, the standards by which we should be guided. The role here of nature means, among other things, that people elsewhere, as well as diverse groups in our own country, can reasonably be appealed to with respect to the most important matters that affect human relations. Nature should help people identify the ugly or the grotesque for what it is.

The standards to be looked to, then, are not limited to our time and place. Nature tends to be put to good use, in our circumstances, in not only Shakespeare but also in the Bible (even though no explicit use of the term *nature* is made either in the Old Testament or in the Gospels). On the other hand, the misguided people I have been talking about, whose atrocities have to be anticipated, often depend upon misreadings of the Bible, of the Constitution (especially its Second and Tenth Amendments), of History, and of Nature herself. At the same time, such people can be offended, and thus can be provoked, by the publicized abuses of nature by the more sophisticated among us.

Nature should also help us retain a sense of proportion in our responses to the calamities we happen to have visited upon us from time to time. Dreadful as the Oklahoma City bombing is, for example, it can be dwarfed in its magnitude, if not in its moral implications, by the number of premature deaths for which drunken drivers, gun distributors, tobacco manufacturers, and Cold Warriors have been responsible among us in recent decades.

Be that as it may, the misguided among us, insofar as they depend upon unexamined opinions, need the help that logic, science, moral teachings, civics lessons, and common sense can provide.

vii.

Also needed for promulgating and maintaining sound opinions among us is, as I have indicated, the promotion of confidence in the prerogatives of the community. Particularly to be countered here are the somewhat fashionable opinions about the illegitimacy of government that we hear all around us. This irresponsible talk contributes to the subversion among us of a sense of citizen discipline.

These unfortunate developments, which can be provoked by heavyhanded if not thoughtless governmental measures, may ultimately depend upon illusions about what is truly one's own. What, in our circumstances, makes any property one's own? We hear more and more about people who consider virtually all taxation to be robbery and virtually all regulation to be enslavement. Yet they want to be protected by expensive armaments from foreign enemies and they want to be provided state-of-the-art highways upon which they can speed in safety.

There may be something childish about much of the current libertarian impulse, an impulse which seems to be growing in strength. Certainly, there are all kinds of illusions abroad in the land today about what we can have and can enjoy on our own. It is not sufficiently appreciated how natural it is for human beings to rely upon the conventions that a community may chance to develop, including the rules it may have about the allocation, sharing and transfer of property.

Also illusory is what various of the "patriots" among us are saying these days about the right of revolution endorsed by the Founders of this country. We are being offered as well, in horrendous displays of one-man campaigns of revenge and destruction, monstrous mockeries of a laudable self-reliance. It is clear both from the Declaration of Independence and from the conduct of the Founders that the right-of-revolution principle looks to the replacement of bad government by good government, not to the elimination of government altogether, the advocacy of which the Founders would have regarded as at best an amiable fantasy and as at worst dangerous nonsense.

viii.

The promulgation and maintenance of sound opinions among us need as well the willingness to place restraints upon what is generally or routinely available in our everyday life.   No doubt, it would be self-defeating in our circumstances to attempt to suppress completely the harmful effects in this country of such things as alcohol, tobacco, automobiles, and firearms. (Our self-defeating war on drugs is instructive here.) On the other hand, it is destructive of the sense of community to deny to the community any role in regulating such things, including (in effect) the opinions we have about them and about our duty and power to deal with them.

Much the same can be said about the harmful effects of the violence and sensuality to which we are routinely subjected in the name of entertainment and news. Insensitivity, if not even perverse appetites, are likely to be developed or at least legitimated by such relentless exposure.

All of these private offerings and private indulgences are compounded in their corrupting effects by what government does to us — at home, by such assaults as the recourse not only to the death penalty but to ever more prisons; abroad, by such assaults as the Vietnam War, which helped undermine faith in government.[65] Nor did the final Waco action, two years to the day before the Oklahoma City bombing, ever make much sense. Were not the deluded criminals besieged in that Branch Davidian compound in effect securely imprisoned by the

---

[65]   See, on capital punishment, Anastaplo, *The American Moralist*, pp. 422-27. See, on the Vietnam War, *ibid.*, pp. 224-44. See, on the Thrasymachean approach to such matters, note 33, above, note 87, below. See, on the war on drugs, Anastaplo, "Governmental Drug-Testing and the Sense of Community," *Nova Law Review*, 11:295 (1987).

government before the attempt was made to take them in hand in order to continue to imprison them?

Symptomatic of the steady weakening of the moral fiber of our people, to which government is contributing, is the growing reliance upon gambling revenues, instead of upon taxation, to finance the services that the community obviously needs. The official promotion of gambling among us encourages people to believe that diligent effort and old-fashioned virtue are not the keys to success and happiness.

ix.

Finally, in this inventory of what is needed for the promulgation and maintenance of sound opinions in this country, there is the understanding of what it means to be truly free. Some of the disaffected among us make much of governmental tyranny, but they are so bedeviled by fear and anger that they cannot see that they have enslaved themselves. Certainly they do not see that one is free only if one thinks, talks and acts as one should.

Self-centeredness must be countered, including that form of it which makes much of fearfulness and self-preservation. Self-interest finds everyday expression among us in our reliance upon a free-market system. That form of economic organization can, with all of its considerable benefits, make ever more people feel vulnerable, especially when technological developments deprive them of the economic and social security which they had once expected.

Both the widespread vulnerability felt and the desperate measures relied upon by all too many of our unduly disturbed fellow-citizens testify to the childishness (the sometimes cruel childishness) that is coming to be fostered by our way of life — and to which irresponsible newspaper publishers and broadcast executives, as well as over-ambitious politicians, contribute. Consider, for example, the amount, as well as the kind, of entertainment (including an excess of commercialized sports) to which we have become addicted. At times, it can seem, even the most violent and destructive "scenarios" that troubled people conjure up and publicize are regarded as no more than still another form of "fun and games." We, as a self-governing citizen body with considerable experience, should know by now how to do much better than all this.

PART THREE

A RETURN TO FUNDAMENTAL QUESTIONS

I.

IS THE SELF GROUNDED IN THE SOUL?[66]

> If one wants to have a taste of death,
> let him sleep with his shoes on.[67]

i.

The noun, *self,* as it is likely to be used by us these days, is defined as "the union of elements ([such] as body, emotions, thoughts, and sensations) that constitute the individuality and identity of a person."[68] Our standard dictionary follows up this definition with a list of some two hundred combinations in which *self* is used, ranging from *self-abasement* through *self-generated* to *self-worshiper.* Thereafter some three hundred additional items are provided, ranging from *self-abandoned* and *self-absorbed* through *self-image, self-interest,* and *selfish* to *self-winding* and *self-worth.*

The same dictionary devotes only a dozen entries to forms of the term *soul,* such as *soul brother, souled, soul food, soulful, soul kiss, soulless,*

---

[66]   This talk was prepared for delivery at the Lenoir-Rhyne College Humanities Conference, Wildacres Conference Center, Little Switzerland, North Carolina, May 18, 1985.

[67]   *The Jewish Encyclopedia* (New York: KTAV Publishing House), vol. 4, p. 486 (*Yoma* 78b).

[68]   The dictionary drawn upon here is *Webster's Ninth New Collegiate Dictionary.*

soul mate, soul music, and *soul-searching. Soul* itself is defined as "the immaterial essence, animating principle, or actuating cause of an individual life." This is followed up with "the spiritual principle embodied in human beings, all rational and spiritual beings, or the universe." It is symptomatic of modern times that so much is made of *self,* compared to *soul,* however intimately these terms may be related.

The relations between these two terms, *self* and *soul,* are suggested by the following observations:

> The *self* is what emerges when much is made of what is called *individuality* among us. (Notice that we do use in this connection the term *self* more than the old-fashioned term, *soul.*) An emphasis upon individuality means, among other things, that we should attempt to intensify the experiences of the self. But, I suggest, if the emphasis is placed upon individuality and its expression, we are bound to have schisms of the soul; indeed, we *should* have such schisms, if only to give each part of the soul something of what it yearns for . . . . [This seems the way, for some, to complete self-fulfillment.]
>
> Is not *soul* critically different from *self?* *Self,* as I have indicated, is somehow intimately related to individuality. *Soul,* on the other hand, points to what is common or general, to a principle, to a natural function, to a standard to be realized. The full development of the soul means a lessening of selfness, or individuality — a conformity of oneself to the very best.[69]

It may follow from these observations that when one's soul is fully developed one's childhood and personal history do not matter much. But such disciplined development (however much it looks to a model or standard of excellence) might be regarded by many moderns as a kind of death, a

---

[69]   Anastaplo, *The Artist as Thinker,* pp. 221, 223.

notion to which we should return on this occasion.

The *self*, at least as we have come to know it, seems to be that which results from the soul's collaboration with the body. Another way of putting this is to say that the self exhibits the effects of the body upon the soul. Still another way of putting this is to say that the self is the soul with certain elements diluted if not even bleached out. The supreme activity of the soul, as once understood, was divine contemplation or philosophical understanding. Insofar as any one grasps the most important things, therefore, he is like all others who grasp those things.

Self, on the other hand, looks more to the particular, the parochial, the personal (including the familial). It can be odd, however, to think of this identifiable entity, or this form of self-consciousness, enduring forever. Terms such as *self-preservation* and *self-sacrifice* contend for preeminence here. This bears upon the pathos that can be heard in the inscription found on John Keats's gravestone in a Roman cemetery: "Here lies one whose name is writ in water." Our particularity is both attractive and vulnerable. Even royalty may have their names forgotten. The recent discovery of the large tomb for dozens of the sons of Ramses II may temporarily revive their memory; but this tomb reminds us of the multitudes of others, royalty as well as peasantry, who have left no individual traces. The soulless self, to which we have become accustomed, tends in its emphasis upon particularity to be unduly materialistic or mechanistic — and as such it tends to make difficult, if not impossible, that form of self-fulfillment found through self-knowing.

I will interweave more or less technical observations about the self and the soul with reminders of what are for us common experiences — our experiences with identical twins, with fatigue, and with old-fashioned movies.   This interweaving is an effort to flesh out my technical observations. I offer thereby a body, or illustrations, which might help us see better the soul, or the principles, of this discourse.[70]

ii.

A couple of weeks ago I saw, across the room from me at a physics lecture, a man with whom I have long had a nodding acquaintance, a man whom I had seen at such lectures before. I nodded; he did not. That left me with a minor mystery. Perhaps he had not noticed me or my greeting. A few minutes later, another man came into the room: *he* was my man. When I saw the "original," the other man was at once exposed as an inadvertent imposter. No nodding back and forth was needed to confirm what I could at once grasp.   This is an experience we have all had, testifying to our remarkable ability to distinguish among the multitudes of particulars by which we happen to be confronted all the time. These two men sat together. Perhaps they were relatives.

My next pair were decidedly relatives, so much so that they could seem to be one person instead of two. They were identical twins, in their sixties perhaps, seated across from me on a Chicago elevated train. Nature and art combined to make each of these women appear the duplicate of the other. Facial features, including coloring of skin and hair, body-build and weight — all seemed the same; style of hair, clothing, shoes and stockings,

---

[70]   See Anastaplo, *Human Being and Citizen*, pp. 87-96 (on the soulless "self"); *The American Moralist*, pp. 3-19, 582-91.

handbags — all were exactly the same. So were the ways they talked, gestured, moved their heads, rose to leave, and walked. They were coordinated in their movements the way birds in flight can be, making it difficult if not impossible for the observer to determine who had taken the lead in any change of course. (It may be worth noticing that neither woman wore a wedding ring.)

So much duplication reflects considerable deliberate effort. There can be something uncanny about such deliberateness, especially when it is likely that it has gone on for five or six decades. At the same time, it is so compulsive a duplication that it hardly looks deliberate. One can wonder whether either of these women can truly be seen so long as the other is present. One can even wonder whether either of them can see her self as separate from the other's.

The following day I happened upon a pair of identical twins just off Michigan Avenue (behind the Tribune Tower). (They seemed to be heading toward the National Broadcasting Company Tower.) Once again, everything was in duplicate — including, perhaps most astonishingly, the crosses marked on their foreheads. It was Ash Wednesday. What makes this astonishing is that Christianity does stand for personal choice, or individuality — and yet here were two women who had evidently moved in tandem, if not in lockstep, from their mother's womb.

These two women were certainly different from the two I had seen the day before elsewhere in the city. But it became impossible for me to *feel* certain about this, whatever the divergences there may have been between the two pairs. That is, I had encountered on successive days two sets of twins who were so much alike in their twinness that I could even wonder if the two pairs had been the same pair — just as one can wonder whether a pair of identical twins is really one person. Twinness becomes so much the dominant characteristic that one pair of twins can be confused with another, at least so long as they are of the same gender and of roughly the same age and size.

It can be sobering, as well as instructive, to be reminded of how much one's material as well as one's social circumstances (including bodily features) matter. Such external identity can affect elements of the soul. We can see here how much determinism, or a kind of mechanism, may figure into what we are and how we conduct ourselves. In what ways, if at all, does each such twin have a will of her own, a self that is truly particular and distinctive? Do not such twins remind us of the determinism that modern science tends to consider decisive, not only in the physical world but also (to a considerable extent) for human beings?[71]

However differentiated most, if not all, people we know may be, the further away in time or space people are, the more alike and undifferentiated they can seem to us. This applies both to the multitudes that die in massacres and famines and to the dozens of sons that Ramses buried during his half-century on the Egyptian throne. A more benign image of this kind of coordination is that of the Rockettes who used to dance in Radio City. I always found peculiar the stories of wealthy men who would take a fancy

---

[71]   Immanuel Kant tried to work out a doctrine of personal responsibility that is compatible with scientific determinism. See, e.g., Anastaplo, *The American Moralist*, pp. 27-32. Does not liberal democracy depend upon the assumption that there are choices to be made and that political as well as personal responsibility follows upon such choices?

to this or that Rockette, even though these women were trained to look so much alike to the masculine eye.

Also peculiar may be what the mass media are doing to whatever commendable individuality our fellow citizens had once had. Is this what is likely to happen to the self when its rootedness in the soul is abandoned? Perhaps many of the disturbances that we encounter these days reflect desperate efforts on the part of people, beginning with youngsters, to come alive by being someone distinguishable from others. (Another pair of identical twins I encountered on the streets of Chicago a fortnight ago were very much like those of an earlier generation that I have described. These two women were in their late twenties. Although everything was again the same — hair style, brown raincoats, shoes and socks, and the way they walked — they did carry their purses and bags on different sides.)

iii.

Before continuing with other common experiences that may throw light on the *self*, I return (however briefly) to a more technical discussion of the matter, beginning with observations from the "Personal Identity" entry in the *Encyclopedia of Philosophy*, where it is said that the word *self* is

> sometimes used to mean the whole series of a person's inner mental states and sometimes, more restrictedly, the spiritual substance to which the philosopher says they belong. The use of the word "self," however, has the effect of confining the question to the unity of the mind and of preventing the answer from relying on the temporal persistence of the body. This has made the unity problem seem intractable, especially when the fleetingness of mental images, feelings, and the like is contrasted with the temporal persistence their owner needs in order even to engage in the relatively lengthy processes of dreaming, reasoning, or scrutinizing the external world.

The dictionary space usually devoted to forms of the term *self*, when compared to that devoted to forms of the term *soul*, testifies (I have suggested) to the modern pre-occupation with self. It is hard to find in ancient Greek a word for *self*.[72] Similar observations might be made about the related modern terms *conscience* and *privacy*.

There is, in the term *self*, an emphasis upon the uniqueness, or specialness, of *me*. If the self is emphasized, dignity becomes critical, and we hear much of privacy and of self-fulfillment. If, on the other hand, the soul is emphasized, virtue becomes critical, and we hear more of citizenship and patriotism — and of the need to avoid corruption of the soul.

There may be seen, in the emergence of the self out of a Christian view of the soul and its personal relation to God, an attempt to add to temporal discourse that divine interest in humanity exhibited in the Bible. Ancient philosophy had not offered to human beings at large what the Bible did. Christianity has emphasized, more than Judaism, the immortality of the soul, which means that the self has its individuality both enhanced and perpetuated forever.

Modern philosophers, such as Hobbes and Descartes (and perhaps Machiavelli), work far more than ancient philosophers did from the interests, if not the autonomy, of the individual. Self-consciousness may even be relied upon as the foundation of all that seems to be known. Radical

---

72   Some try to use the Greek word *psychos* for *self*, but that is not right. Perhaps a variation of *autos* would be possible. See the opening words of Plato's *Phaedo*. In Latin, a variation of *persona*, or mask, might be used. When we use *psyche*, we look more to passions which should be ministered to than to any model by which the soul (including its passion) should be guided.

inwardness, which may hold the seeds of madness, does promise certainty about the things that can be known, things related to one's awareness of one's own existence, perhaps also of one's self-interest.[73]

When individuality is at the core both of philosophy and of political action, much more is likely to be made of self-expression as the source of the greatest satisfaction, with the common good and a sense of excellence being displaced as the end of liberty. (Another form of this may be the self-assertion advocated by Martin Heidegger, however learned he may have been about ancient things.) The old-fashioned approach, on the other hand, had the thoughtful man recognizing that the more thoughtful he is, the less likely he is to be unique or "individual" or indeed mortal. That is, he recognizes that "he" has been, as thinker, "here" "before," and that "he" will "return." Only the accidental and essentially superfluous is "individual" and hence vulnerable. Philosophers, then, tend to resemble one another — but not in the way that my identical twins do. It may even be said that that which is most significantly immortal in the universe is the reasoning being who contemplates the principles of things, not the individual characterized by chance, errors, and personal attachments.[74] Still, people who are taught

---

[73]   See, e.g., Anastaplo, *Human Being and Citizen*, p. 220; *The Artist as Thinker*, p. 224; *The American Moralist*, pp. 86-87.

[74]   See, e.g., Anastaplo, *Human Being and Citizen*, p. 317, n.4; *The American Moralist*, p. 137. See, on Martin Heidegger, *ibid.*, p. 144; Horst Mewes, "Leo Strauss and Martin Heidegger: Greek Antiquity and the Meaning of Modernity," in Peter Graf Kielmansegg, Horst Mewes, and Elisabeth Glaser-Schmidt, eds., *Hannah Arendt and Leo Strauss* (New York: Cambridge University Press, 1995), p. 105.

> Yet while according to Plato and Aristotle *to be* in the highest sense means to be *always*, Heidegger contends that *to be* in the highest sense means *to exist*, that

to make as much as we do of both liberty and equality are apt to resist arguments which not only urge restraints upon us but also consider some states of the soul inferior to others. This can mean that it is more important to be oneself than it is to be good. Modern economic as well as political conditions permit, if they do not even promote self-expression. In short, that which is the best among human beings is not the unique or the individual, but rather that which most resembles the Good.[75]

By now you have probably again become tired of more or less technical observations. It is time, then, to return to something more familiar — and it is appropriate that that should be concerned with the all-too-common experience of fatigue.

iv.

Fatigue, when examined properly, can help us see what both the body and the soul contribute to what is known as the self. The body may be most in evidence when it is defective or exhausted. Some may argue that the body is even more in evidence when one is engaged in erotic relations

---

is to say, *to be* in the manner in which man *is*: *to be* in the highest sense is constituted by mortality.

Leo Strauss, *The Rebirth of Classical Political Rationalism* (Chicago: University of Chicago Press, 1989), p. 37. See, also, notes 78 and 86, below.

[75]   See, on distinctly modern terms, Anastaplo, *The American Moralist*, p. 142. See, on conscience, *ibid.*, p. 133; *Human Being and Citizen*, p. 275. See, on the self, *ibid.*, p. 90; *The Artist as Thinker*, p. 403 n. 112; *The American Moralist*, p. 230. See, on self-expression, *Human Being and Citizen*, p. 135; *The Artist as Thinker*, p. 6. See, on individuality and virtue, *Human Being and Citizen*, p. 293 n. 13. See, on individuality and immortality, *ibid.*, p. 317 n. 4. See, on privacy, *The American Moralist*, p. 230. See, on Machiavelli and individuality, *The Artist as Thinker*, p. 438 n. 194. See, on the relation between the Good and the unique, *ibid.*, pp. 413 n. 145, 431 n. 175.

— but what makes erotic relations most engaging are elements that are not physical. When one is not tired, one simply makes use of one's body without noticing it. (It is like the experience of seeing things: the soul sees, or so it seems, not the eyes.)

Fatigue can not only keep one from being able to do certain things; it can also sap one of the will to try to do those things, so much so as to induce a kind of heaviness if not even depression. Things can sometimes appear hopeless, with one's ability to think clearly impaired. Mistakes in recollection, calculation, and judgment can result. It is encouraging in such circumstances to recall that one has felt this way before and that a short nap, or if need be, a night's rest, can make all the difference in the world.[76]

Fatigue, then, may have its uses, including the obvious one of requiring the body to be replenished and restored to the working order most useful for the soul. (We anticipate here the problem of whether the soul can function as soul if there is not a body for it to work through, and not only when dealing with the material universe.) Another, however unnoticed, use of fatigue is that of permitting us to see how the soul does differ from the body, especially when one finds oneself wanting to do things that the body is not up to, at least for the moment. (An illness is, in a sense, a kind of extended fatigue.) That is, fatigue can help or permit one to see past one's body — to see what is essential, or what is best, in one's total makeup.

Something odd can happen in these circumstances. I have found, when I have turned to studying my own fatigue, that I am not hampered in

---

[76] See Anastaplo, *The Artist as Thinker*, p. 291; *Human Being and Citizen*, pp. 219, 316 n. 2.

the same way (or to the same degree) by fatigue as I am when studying other things that my fatigue keeps me from pursuing for the moment. Indeed, fatigue tends to be lifted somewhat when I examine fatigue itself — as if fatigue wants to exclude examination. A kind of refreshment, if only temporarily and for limited purposes, can result.

Be that as it may, does not the soul assert itself in such a process, as something that exists somewhat independently of the body and hence of the fatigue that the body is susceptible to? Indeed, is not the soul as such never fatigued, especially if it is purified, or in the process of being purified, of ignorance and of desires and attachments that are associated with its own and other bodies?

v.

Much more can no doubt be said about the workings of fatigue, a condition which may be an anticipation of the process of dying. Fortunately, however, the lessons one can learn from fatigue about the relations between soul and body do not depend upon serious illness or old age when death appears imminent. I trust that enough has been said by me about fatigue, at least for the moment, in this effort to suggest what the soul is like independent of the body, that soul which is apt to be neglected in modern accounts of the self.

It is only prudent, however, to acknowledge again the apparent need of the soul for *some* body with which to associate itself. This has to be done lest one be carried away by the notion that the sooner a soul can divest itself of its body, the sooner that soul can come to its full realization. A precious perfume may be worth much more than the glass bottle which contains it. But, so far as we know, some bottle is needed if the perfume is not to be dissipated and lose its effectiveness. Is it the same for the soul in its relation to some body?

Even so, death (or the collapse of the body) poses much more of a threat to the self than it does to the soul. For the self, I have argued, depends much more upon the individual and hence the accidental than does the soul — and this means that a body is critical not only for the existence of the self (as it may be for the practical existence of the soul) but also for the special form of the self. That is, the soul can sometimes rise above its body in a way, or to a degree, that the self cannot.

vi.

The self is illuminated not only when the body undergoes the debilitation of fatigue or serious illness, but also when it is furthest from that condition — that is, when the body is fresh and vital, even more so when the body is beautiful. Again, we can refresh ourselves by turning from a technical discussion to a reliance upon something familiar, in this case, a film classic which I happened to see recently, *National Velvet*.

A youthful Elizabeth Taylor (Velvet) is devoted to a horse; a youthful Mickey Rooney is devoted to her — and is persuaded by her to help prepare her horse to compete in the Grand National. Velvet herself (albeit incognito) has to ride the horse in England's premier race — and we are prepared to see her win it, whatever the rules ordain thereafter.

The collaboration of body and soul depicted in this movie points to a peak, or to what seems to be a peak. Beautiful bodies (both human and animal) are used to suggest virtuous souls, reminding us that the beautiful is in some way a promise of the good. We are reminded also of how art relies upon the use of bodies in order to talk about souls.

We are reminded as well — and this can be sad here — we are reminded of the limits of this collaboration of body and soul when we reflect upon what has happened as adults to both of these gifted child actors. These attractive young people knew how to *look* good but, if the stories one hears about them are to be believed, they never learned how to *be* good. Evidently, they could not see their own movie, and be lifted up by it, in the way that the typical movie-goer might have been.

Critical to the way these actors and their director proceeded were the images that were presented on the screen, images of the virtues upon which the effectiveness of this movie depends. Decisive here is not the condition of the soul of any actor but rather the *persona* that is offered to the public. It is the elevation, as well as the concealment, of the person that is vital to the modern notion of the self. That may be one reason why we have so many celebrities and so few great-souled men and women to contemplate.[77]

vii.

We depend upon our poets, as well as upon the occasional philosopher, to remind us of what we somehow know about the soul and its relation to the body. The philosopher's efforts here *are* apt to be technical and hence not easily profited from or even endured by most people. The artist, on the other hand, can be memorable in what he presents us, however

---

[77] See, on the limitations of the cinema, Anastaplo, *The Artist as Thinker*, pp. 322-30; *The American Moralist*, p. 245. See, also, Anastaplo, "Can Beauty 'Hallow Even the Bloodiest Tomahawk'?," *The Critic*, Winter 1993, p. 2.

much that presentation may require analysis for its full appreciation.

The workings of the soul, with a minimum of reliance upon the body, may be discerned in a story told by Mark Twain in *Life on the Mississippi* (Chapter XI) about a veteran pilot's taking a steamboat through a difficult passage on the River. This pilot had entered the pilot-house, during a night that was "particularly drizzly, sullen, and dark," to offer to replace the pilot who was on duty, saying,

> Let me take her, George; I've seen this place since you have, and it is so crooked that I reckon I can run it myself easier than I could tell you how to do it.

To this the other pilot replied,

> It is kind of you, and I swear *I* am willing. I haven't got another drop of perspiration left in me. I have been spinning around and around the wheel like a squirrel. It is so dark I can't tell which way she is swinging till she is coming around like a whirligig.

The relieved pilot stayed on in the pilot-house to watch his colleague work, finally exclaiming upon being shown a "marvel of steering," "Well, I though I knew how to steer a steamboat, but that was another mistake of mine." Even more remarkable displays of the pilot's art thereafter moved the professional observer to proclaim, "That's the sweetest piece of piloting that was ever done on the Mississippi River! I wouldn't believe it could be done, if I hadn't seen it."

Well, it turns out, this marvelous piloting was done by a man caught up in a fit of sleepwalking. Others are appalled upon learning what had happened, but the pilot who had witnessed the feats of his colleague pronounces this magisterial judgment:

> Well, I think I'll stay by next time he has one of those fits. But I hope
> he'll have them often. You just ought to have seen him take this boat
> through Helena crossing. *I* never saw anything so gaudy before. And if
> he can do such gold-leaf, kid-glove, diamond-breastpin piloting when he
> is sound asleep, what *couldn't* he do if he was dead!

We *can* imagine this episode happening as it is described, with the soul of the sleepwalking pilot exerting itself unencumbered by the inhibitions that might ordinarily have been prompted by the body's sense of its vulnerability. Even so, our laughter, upon hearing "logical deduction" carried to this extreme — "An if he can do such . . . piloting when he is sound asleep, what *couldn't* he do if he was dead!" — our laughter testifies to our natural awareness that (so far as we can tell from our experience) the human does depend upon a living body, however much the soul rises above it on occasion.

Still, it may be prudent, in a materialistic age when catering to the *self* prevails, to err ont he side of making too little of the *body*, thereby making it more likely that the *soul* will be given its due.[78]

---

[78]   If the body is made too much of, a preoccupation with self-preservation is likely to develop, thereby making the best in us more vulnerable than it should be. See note 74, above. See, on death and dying, Anastaplo, *Human Being and Citizen*, pp. 214-21. Compare note 82, below.

II.

ARE THE MORAL VIRTUES GROUNDED IN NATURE?[79]

Man is by nature a political animal: therefore, even when [human beings] need no assistance from one another, they no less want to live together. Not but that the common advantage also brings them together, to the extent to which it contributes a share for each of noble living. Now then this is most of all the end both for all in common and separately; but they also come together and hold the political community together for the sake of living itself; for perhaps there is some portion of the noble in life even as it is by itself alone, so long as the hardships of life are not too excessive. And it is clear that most men endure much evil suffering, clinging to life, as if in life itself there is a certain serenity and natural sweetness.

— Aristotle[80]

i.

Are the moral virtues grounded in nature? The common understanding of the three terms I have just used — *moral virtues, nature,* and *grounded* — suffices for our immediate purpose. It is on the basis of that understanding that our question first engages us.

---

[79] This talk was prepared for delivery to the Center for Christianity and the Common Good, The University of Dallas, Irving, Texas, September 15, 1995. Preparation of this talk was aided considerably by conversations with Laurence Berns, Victor Gourevitch, and Harry V. Jaffa. See, for a related University of Dallas talk (September 17, 1995, Anastaplo, "On the Sacred and the Profane: The Flag Desecration Amendment," *Congressional Record*, October 18, 1995, p. E1965.

[80] Aristotle, *Politics* 1278b18-29 (Laurence Berns translation).

This question is an ancient one. But this question may be intensified and otherwise dramatized by modern science.

Nature, as it has long been understood, is consistent with the notion of the eternity of the universe. This notion is reinforced, or made more likely (at least "psychologically"), by the vast extent of time and space that modern science lays out before us.

Related to this notion of the eternity of the universe is the considerable evidence offered us for the accidental origins of the human race (as well as of other species here on earth). The substantial anatomical similarity between other species and the human species is taken for granted by biologists and other such scientists. We notice in passing that we do not consider the other species of which we know to have much if anything to do with the moral virtues, however much what they do, or "ought to do," may be grounded in nature.

The more that is made of evolution, the more likely it seems to the modern scientist that the origins of the human species depended upon somewhat fortuitous combinations of matter. (This is consistent with the radically materialistic bent of modern science.) These material combinations (about which physics, chemistry, and other sciences have much to say) make it possible, if not likely, that our passions and appetites (with which the moral virtues are very much concerned) are in large due to material causes.

These currently pervasive opinions suggest, in some quarters, that there may have been other origins of life elsewhere in the vast reaches of the universe. Cautions are heard about the exceedingly rare combination of material factors that permits life to emerge and sustain itself. But may there not be forms of life that we can do little more than image, if even that? Those who believe in angels, for example, cannot tell us much, if anything, about their "chemistry."

The possibility of life elsewhere in the universe (aside, of course, from what may be found in the Inferno, Purgatory, and Paradise) is no longer dismissed as merely fanciful. That is, it is said, the vastness of the universe (in both time and space) makes other life possible if not even likely here and there. What is not said as often is that that very vastness makes physical contact between those loci of life virtually impossible.

Such are the scientific findings and speculations that tend to undermine the traditional reliance upon revelation ministering to the guidance and care of one particular species of immortal souls. The significance not only of individual human souls but even of the human species can become harder to take seriously whenever our scientists tell us about millions upon millions of galaxies, among which even our galaxy (to say nothing of our solar system) can seem inconsequential.

What difference does it make, and to whom, how other rational beings conduct themselves, especially in circumstances when we are not immediately or personally concerned? This is related to questions about the goodness or enduring worth of personal conduct that no one else ever learns about. Another way of putting this is to wonder whether a study of nature may help our understanding, not our judgment, leading to the possibility that the only reliable grasp of things by human beings may be intellectual, not moral.

Still another way of putting all this is to ask what difference it makes now what was thought, said, or done by the immeasurable multitudes of "persons" we can be fairly sure lived, on the earth alone if not elsewhere, at various times in the past. What, if anything, does the kind of expansion of the human perspective of time and space to which we have become accustomed do to our ability and willingness to regard the moral virtues as grounded in nature — or as matters to be taken seriously by the dispassionate observer? May not the movements of long-gone stars and planets be both easier to understand and more interesting?

ii.

Let us come back down to earth by considering our opening question from a much more limited everyday perspective, however much that perspective may be influenced by the remarkable cosmological speculations of our day.

What, then, should or does guide us in what we do? To some extent (at times, to a considerable extent) we are moved by pleasure and pain. Related to this is the desire for self-preservation (or, at least, the desire to avoid an early or a painful death). This can be keyed to personal advantage or to communal advantage (or to both).

We have already noticed that if a species had not had this desire for self-preservation, it probably would not have developed or have been able to perpetuate itself. A pain/pleasure guidance related to this desire is seen in the other species as well — and it has many benefits, as well as creating problems. Biologists find it useful to approach instinctive conduct as it were purposive, serving the overall interests of the species if not also of the individual.

Arguments are rarely needed to persuade the typical human being to seek and accept pleasures or to avoid and reduce pains. A few severely inhibited people may have to be encouraged to let themselves enjoy now and then the pleasures available to them. Arguments are much more likely to be needed to encourage, if not even to require, someone to forego certain pleasures and to undergo certain pains. We even have to learn that some immediate pleasures can lead to severe pains or can deprive us of other pleasures. It is in the arguments here that morality, as ordinarily understood, can come to view.

iii.

The enjoyment of pleasure, if not also the reduction of pain, may be seen in its most satisfying, if not in its more enduring form, in the activity of the genuine philosopher. Other kinds of activities may be regarded by others as more enjoyable. But, it can be argued, only those who have had some experience of the various kinds of activities can reliably rank them with a view to what they contribute to a general satisfaction with one's life and to an effective use of one's talents.

The most serious competition for philosophy, at least among worldly pursuits, is offered by the political life and its ambitions. But the pleasure available in politics may be too dependent upon others to be reliable — and for this, and other reasons, it may be illusory.[81]

---

[81]   Consider, for example, the bitterness of Alexander the Great in India when his men would go no further toward the Great Sea.

Many would look to bodily gratifications, and especially sexuality, as the source of the most intense, all-engrossing pleasures. But this sort of pleasure is notoriously brief — and all too often does not deliver what it promises. Even so, there is a *knowing* element in sexuality, which is related perhaps to the long-recognized role of *eros* in philosophy.

In addition, sexuality may help us learn what knowing is, including the self-confident knowing of ourselves. In any event, it is critical to the ability to learn and to know that one's soul be in proper shape and that one know oneself well enough to make allowances for one's limitations.

The ranking of the various pursuits, by those who have experienced enough of each to be able to judge, extends also to the subject-matters investigated by the inquiring mind. There is, it comes to be believed, something intrinsic to various subjects, with some perceivable as higher and others as lower. Both the solver of crossword puzzles and the cosmologist work with "wholes" (as well as with holes) — but is it not obvious to most of us which pursuit is intrinsically higher?

Nature provides, or at least seems to provide, guidance as to what it means to know and as to what premises and forms of reasoning are needed for learning and knowing. The supernatural may also be instructive here — but that is beyond my jurisdiction, at least on this occasion.

iv.

We have reminded ourselves of the pleasures and pains (or limitations) of the body and also of the mind. We can now turn directly to the critical question of the status of, or the grounding for, the moral virtues.

Is there a sense of moral goodness that is not keyed to or in the service primarily of either personal or communal interests and advantages? Is there, in short, a basis in nature for morality?

If nature *is* at work here, the human being may be inclined or directed toward morality without appreciating how or why this is so. Our question may appear, then, as largely "theoretical." But how we answer it may affect how morality, or the law dependent upon and serving morality, is regarded, so much so in some circumstances as to subvert the hold upon a people of their established morality. The opinions here of a few may have profound consequences, if not immediately, at least in the long run.

This inquiry can become acute if there should be an undermining of conventions and tradition (or the old way) with respect to morality by modern science. There has long been recognized to be a tension between the pursuit of justice (or the common good) and the quest for truth.

Be that as it may, is there something about morality that provides pleasures in somewhat the way that there are pleasures of the body (whether personal or communal) and pleasures of the mind or soul (whether in the form of philosophy or of theology)? Or is there something about morality that provides an attraction which is superior to pleasure in whatever form?

The pleasures related to the exercise of the moral virtues may be more complicated than the pleasures of the body or those of the mind or soul. Are the pleasures associated with the moral virtues sometimes less selfish than those other pleasures — and hence, in a sense, more questionable? That the pleasures of the moral virtues may be more complicated is suggested by the fact that those virtues are devoted, or are related, to the blending of body and soul.[82]

v.

To recapitulate: There are pleasures of the body that may be enjoyed with little or no thinking required. This may be observed in all kinds of living things, as well as in what happens to and with our bodies as we sleep. Even so, the mind may be very much required for, as well as involved in, the more interesting bodily pleasures.

There are pleasures of the soul or mind which are expected for the incorporeal soul (for example, in Heaven) — and which we can experience somewhat here on earth, forgetting (at least for awhile) our bodies, time, place, and other circumstances.

What, if any, basis is there for morality in nature? A digression may be of some use here. What does it matter how this question is answered or, at least, what is said here by us? Aside from the question of whether morality is grounded in nature, there is the question of whether nature herself should be obeyed, assuming that nature makes her guidance known.[83]

Does not nature makes us "feel" that we should obey her? Is it right or necessary that we should obey? Should we do so "only" because nature

---

[82]   If the body and the soul of the human being cannot exist separately, is the soul directed in its conduct by nature (if only because of the body, which is constantly shaped by nature)? See note 78, above.

[83]   See, e.g., Joseph Cropsey, *Political Philosophy and the Issues of Politics* (Chicago: University of Chicago Press, 1977), pp. 221-30.

moves us to do so? If we "cannot help acting" one way or another, where is the moral element in that action?

Enough, at least for the moment, for this digression. What if any basis *is* there for morality in nature? there is a natural basis for morality in the sense that nature provides physical equipment, parts of the soul, and perhaps inclinations and instincts which make us open to moral considerations and guidance.

This openness seems to be largely, if not exclusively, confined on earth to human beings among the living things which we know by direct observation. Nature permits human beings to use moral teachings, including the curbing of the enjoyment of certain pleasures, to serve various ends. This does suggest that there is something intrinsic to human beings that makes them open to moral teachings, whatever its sources. But what does nature herself "say" about the sources of morality?

An inquiry as to sources is related to what the rules are and to why we should obey those rules. We have anticipated what is sometimes said, even by quite respectable students of this subject: that morality is primarily if not exclusively instrumental or ministerial, that it is not something worth having or exercising for its own sake. Thus, it can be said by those who do consider the intellectual virtues (or the philosophic life) to be grounded in nature, that the moral virtues permit the ordering of society in such a way as to provide philosophers the means and opportunity to work.

Is nihilism implicit in this approach, the approach of distinctively modern thinkers, with an awareness of an abyss all about us? Less of a problem, in a sense, is the thoroughgoing nihilist for whom not even philosophy means much if anything. That is, such a nihilist is both harder and easier to deal with here. We put him[84] to one side, addressing instead those who do recognize a grounding in nature for philosophy but not for morality.

Is the modern philosophic position here one consequence of the modern insistence upon a perhaps unprecedented degree of certainty in all subjects of inquiry? Is moral discourse incapable of appearing precise and hence certain enough for the modern? (We are not concerned here with whether the moral virtues are as high as the intellectual or philosophic virtues, but rather with whether the moral virtues have any grounding in nature.)

Much can be said for the proposition that the moral virtues are instrumental, especially since various of the virtues do depend upon conventions or have obvious practical consequences. That is, no matter what the sources or impulse or motivation in morality, conventions and consequences are often critical in determining what should be done. For example, several virtues depend upon how property or wealth is dealt with — and what *is* property and what may be done with it very much depend upon ever-changing laws. Furthermore, the decent human being respects others' opinions to a considerable extent, avoiding as much as possible being "offensive."[85]

---

[84]   The nihilist *is* much more apt to be male than female. See, on women and nature, Anastaplo, *The American Moralist*, pp. 349-63.

[85]   Aristotle, for one, was aware of the variability of justice. But if there is a best regime, would justice be as variable there as Aristotle recognizes it to be in the everyday world?

Those who argue for the primarily instrumental character of the moral virtues sometimes refer to obviously thoughtful men who are said to endorse this argument.[86] But when one happens to observe such a man close up, what does one see? He can pronounce moral judgments — sometimes about ancient or long-past events or actors, sometimes about Twentieth Century events (such as what the Nazis did in their death camps), and sometimes about people we know personally — such a man can pronounce moral judgments in such a way as not to seem to regard morality as merely instrumental. A genuine moral feeling, as if grounded in nature, is expressed, sometimes spontaneously (that is, evidently without artifice).

Besides, when we consider someone such as Socrates, for whom the life of the inquiring philosopher seemed the life most worthy of the human being, we remember that he was prepared on more than one occasion to sacrifice his life (and hence the opportunity to continue philosophizing here on earth) for the sake of moral rectitude. This seems to represent an endorsement of the moral virtues for their own sake, something that the truly thoughtful men of our time are bound to respect.

Furthermore, there is a problem in regarding the intellectual virtues to be grounded in nature but not the moral virtues. The philosopher's honesty and willingness to run risks in pursuit of the truth seem to have

---

[86]   See, e.g., Shadia B. Drury, *The Political Ideas of Leo Strauss* (New York: St. Martin's Press, 1988). Compare Anastaplo, "Shadia Drury on 'Leo Strauss,'" *The Vital Nexus* (Institute of Human Values, Halifax, Nova Scotia), vol. 1, pp. 9-15 (May 1990). See, also, note 74, above.

some of the characteristics of the moral virtues.[87] In addition, if the intellectual virtues do depend somewhat upon an erotic element, what guides that element? Is it guided in the interest of nature-grounded philosophy — and if so does nature indirectly shape the erotic? The erotic, in any event, may connect the realm of the intellectual virtues to the realm of the moral virtues.

We have been taught that we cannot see certain actions if we do not grasp and take seriously the moral element in those actions. But how seriously can moral virtues be taken if they are regarded as merely instrumental? Consider as well the *noble*, that which is worth having and savoring for its own sake. Is it that which makes it easier for us to see that it is better for someone to be treated unjustly than to be unjust himself?[88]

vi.

However all this may be, there are difficulties, if not risks, in considering morality as primarily instrumental, especially if this opinion becomes widely accepted.

For one thing, morality cannot be effectively instrumental if it is understood to be merely instrumental. We want morality to be regarded as more than instrumental if only because we sense that morality is important,

---

[87]   Thomas Aquinas spoke of prudence as the only intellectual virtue that presupposes the moral virtues. See Anastaplo, "On Freedom," pp. 681-82.

[88]   Will Rogers is quoted as saying, "They may call me a rube and a hick, but I'd rather be the man who bought the Brooklyn Bridge than the man who sold it." Brian Downes, "Will Rogers' Oklahoma," *Chicago Tribune*, July 30, 1995, sec. 12, p. 1. See, also, Anastaplo, "On Crime, Criminal Lawyers, and O. J. Simpson."

that it is vulnerable, and that it is most effective when it is regarded as grounded in nature (or, to somewhat the same effect, in revelation).

Our deepest concerns here may reflect an instinctive (or natural) opening in us to morality. That is, to recognize what we have said about the appeal of the moral virtues is to recognize some grounding in nature for them. This recognition may be required if there is to be an effective response to the challenges posed by Thrasymachus in Book I of Plato's *Republic* and by Glaucon and Adeimantus in Book II. Those challenges suggest that "everyone knows" that if one can get away with injustice, with no one else ever knowing of it, one may seem to have the best of both worlds: others are respectful of justice (which helps your security), while you enjoy things that would not otherwise be available to you.

"Be realistic," we are told by those who believe they know what it is that truly moves people. But, I have suggested, there may be a naturally moral component to facing up to the truth. Those who regard the intellectual virtues as grounded in nature probably rely somewhat upon the moral virtues in the conduct and assessment of the inquiries which the intellectual virtues require and glory in.[89]

If morality is not grounded in nature, then is it at best instrumental, borrowing its dignity from the activity it may happen to serve? Thus, morality would be grounded in nature, but only indirectly, in that it is in the

---

[89]   Furthermore, do not the positions, in Plato's *Republic*, of Thrasymachus and of Glaucon/Adeimantus somehow draw upon something natural in us? Intellectual honesty is invoked and relied upon by them, as if that is something we should all respect. See note 65 above.

service of natural desires (whether of the body or of the mind). Thus, also, it would have no intrinsic dignity.

If morality is indeed something to be used, does not that tend to make the will paramount? The decisiveness of the will in human (if not also in divine) affairs is perhaps distinctively modern.[90] Critical here seems to be the opinion that man makes everything, including his "values." This opinion is reinforced by the growing awareness, partly because of modern science and technology, of the variety of ways of human life around the world.

vii.

What do the varieties of conventions show, those varieties which seem so much the manifestations of chance in human life and which are made so much of by "realists"? However varied these conventions may be, do not their similarities suggest that there may be something natural at work here?

First, there is the very fact that almost all, if not all, communities have moral guides, as if they are intrinsic to human beings.

Second, there is a remarkable compatibility among the many moral codes around the world, even for peoples who were not in touch with each other during their formative stages. Critical divergences in a code here or there may depend upon chance circumstances. but we can usually see the

---

[90]   In American law this opinion may be seen developed in the writings of Oliver Wendell Holmes Jr. and in cases such as *Erie Railroad Company* v. *Tompkins*, 304, U.S. 64 (1938). See William T. Braithwaite, "The Common Law and the Judicial Power: An Introduction to *Swift-Erie*," in *Law and Philosophy*, vol. II, p. 774; Anastaplo, *The Constitution of 1787*, pp. 124, 136; *The Amendments to the Constitution*, p. 458 (*Erie* entry). See, also, note 74, above, note 91, below.

sense of most rules in the circumstances in which we find them. Thus, there is sometimes available an indication of what the basis was, in a particular community, of the determination to adopt the moral code relied upon, a basis which includes elements that we can recognize as defensible if not even as praiseworthy. This, too, can help us to get to the roots of a moral code.

Third, there is the prevalence of the notion that one should be moral, whatever the specifics of the morality of a time or place may be. When some conventions are questioned, this is usually done on the basis of moral standards that are generally accepted. We can even be troubled by someone who casually disregards the morals of his time and place, even when we have reservations about those morals.

Often, of course, the moral code of a people is rooted in some form of revelation. Which revelation governs where may be largely a matter of chance (except, it should be conceded, for the true revelation). No doubt, acceptance of revelation may be in part due to ignorance and fear, if not also to glimpses of the abyss. But there may also be a natural appetite for revelation — or for that which revelation provides, a comprehensive view of the whole. It may be related to that natural desire to know of which Aristotle spoke.

A caution may be in order here. Must not care be taken in making use of revelation (or of any other expression of will) to support rules of conduct, lest that use undermine the grounding of morality in nature? Is not nature useful in shaping us, including our religious associations and other communities, day in and day out? Care must be taken, that is, lest religion come to be regarded as little more than a super-convention.

And if, as happens in the course of centuries to all but perhaps the true religion, purported revelations here and there come to be questioned and replaced, what becomes of the status of morality? One problem here is suggested by the tendency among us today to see a public promotion of morality as a way of foisting religion upon the citizen body.

Nature may express herself through the Believer, even when the Believer no longer considers Nature sufficient. (We can hear talk, for example, of a fallen nature.) Does the Believer, like the modern Realist, tend to undermine reliance upon nature? Does the Believer tend to believe that, without revelation, life is somehow meaningless, hopeless, if not even dangerous? That is, he does not sense the natural basis of morality — or perhaps even the intrinsic goodness of the rational life.

And does the Believer, like the modern Scientist, make too much of the tenuousness of the human species (absent divine providence)? What is the significance of the fact, if fact it is, that all we have and can know, and even the possibility of knowing, is temporary and provisional, with everything that we depend upon (including memory) doomed to disintegration and annihilation?

Yet if matter/energy is eternal, then is not the potential always "here" for "us" to appear again and again? That is, is there not something natural about our very being, including our aspirations, however fortuitous any particular appearance of a species may be?

viii.

We should not conclude this inquiry without noticing the question of what the basis is of the choice of a moral code when rules of conduct are offered as divine commands (or as super-conventions).

If such a code is contrived by human beings, there may be either delusions or deliberate deception at work there. In either case, the moral integrity or worth of the enterprise can be suspected — unless there is a noble lie involved here, which may be salutary in its effects as well as in its intention. Besides, does even the invention of goods reflect a divine spark or urge in human beings, something that is naturally there in both the prophet (or poet) and his audience?

If a moral code is truly from God, there is still the question of how God chooses what He does. It need not be — indeed, probably should not be — considered as arbitrary. Should that to which God looks in framing a moral code be different from that for which nature, in its perfection, also provides.[91]

If divine intervention is put to one side, what does a finite earthly existence, with no prospect of immortal life, do to our sense of meaningfulness of life here? It may depend partly upon whether the appetite for immortal life and salvation is not natural but rather cultivated, and if so how.

---

[91]   See, e.g., Thomas Aquinas, *On Truth*, Q. 23, A. 6, c; Anastaplo, *The American Moralist*, p. 139. Even for nature, character means more than such material factors as geography and genetics. See note 46, above.

Thus, we have moved on this occasion from asking whether morality is good in itself to whether a mortal life (with nothing following personally) is good in itself? These may be related questions. Have not human beings always had the sense that existence is a good thing, absent great calamities and pains? If we are naturally attracted to human life, are we not also naturally drawn to the moral code which evidently makes that life work well and be well?

ix.

Our inquiry on this occasion into the natural basis for morality could well inspire us to wonder whether there is something immoral in questioning the natural basis for morality (unless perhaps one insists at the same time upon the divine basis of morality). That is, if there *is* a natural basis for morality, is there something wrong (morally or intellectually or both) with those who explicitly deny such a basis?

Thus, we can wonder whether there is something deeply wrong with those who are not simply open to the good. Do some intellectuals "allow" their speculative appetites to overcome their moral sensibilities?

Ultimately critical here may be the question whether there is *an idea of the good* that guides all actions as well as all serious inquiry and thought. We recall the opening passage of the *Nicomachean Ethics* and the *Politics*, with their insistence that every pursuit is thought to aim at some good. If Aristotle is correct in what he says there, does not that suggest a natural opening in human beings to the good — and hence to the moral virtues? The virtues, if seen thus, may not be simply instrumental, however much they inform practice.

Even our pleasures and pains continually teach us, or illustrate for us, the idea of the good. Is not that idea vital to the philosophic inquiry which some do concede to be grounded in nature, reinforcing thereby that enduring sense of rightness which moral choices naturally seem to us to rest upon and to serve?

At the very least then, there may be nothing wrong, depending upon how one goes about it, in affirming, or reaffirming, the natural basis for a proper morality.

George Anastaplo is
Lecturer in the Liberal Arts
at the University of Chicago
Professor Emeritus of Political Science and of Philosophy
at Rosary College
and Professor of Law
at Loyola University of Chicago.